pursepective

pursepective

FROM RUIN TO RESILIENCE: A HANDBOOK FOR REBUILDING YOUR LIFE

Dr. Amy M. Cannatta

ISBN: 1507598467
ISBN 13: 9781507598467

The events in this book actually happened. Some of the names and identifying details of some of the characters have been changed to protect the individuals' privacy.

This book is dedicated to my grandmother, Henrietta. Her life was an example of how to lead with resilience and think outside the box to solve life's problems. May her legacy live on through this book.

Contents

Acknowledgments

A SPECIAL THANK YOU TO my daughters for being my compass through life. Without the two of you, I do not know where I would be. Being a mother and role model to both of you is what kept me going through my darkest days when I could have easily just given up.

To my boyfriend, Matt, who is a dream come true and has loved me back to life. You constantly and consistently go above and beyond what any other human being would do to support me, my business, and this important message to share with other victims. Words cannot express how much you mean to me, nor can I even begin to repay all of the support, unpaid website work, and late nights you spent out of sheer devotion and unconditional love for me.

To my mother, who loves me no matter what. You have endured many traumas in life and have somehow managed to maintain your sense of humor.

To my friends, family, and patients reading this. The truth about my inner struggles must be painful for you to read. It has taken me a long time to break my silence about these things. Thank you for understanding and not judging me.

To my friends Mary, Mica, and Casey from chiropractic school, who helped me through my darkest days. The three of you pulled me out of the black hole I thought I had fallen into. You are the three most incredibly inspiring and empowered women I know. The three of you not only saved my life but my daughters' lives as well, and for that I am eternally grateful.

To the editing and layout team at CreateSpace and Sarah, my direct contact, thank you for guiding me and holding my hand throughout this adventure toward becoming a published author.

To Bess and Sarah of WinterCricket Design for giving the book a beautiful and luxurious cover. You're both worth way more than I can pay either of you. Thank you from the bottom of my heart.

To all of my supporters both in person and those of you on social media. Thank you for all of your input on the cover, comments, tweets, likes, shares, and encouragement for this book.

And last but not least, a special acknowledgment to victims and survivors of domestic violence and abuse, whether you are male or female. You are all inspirations to me and reasons for writing this book. We are in this fight together and can make an impact on awareness to break the silence and stop the shame.

Don't judge a book by its cover!

The journey of a thousand miles begins with one step.
—Lao Tzu

I am the master of my fate and the captain of my destiny.
—Nelson Mandela

Preface

WHAT IS YOUR ARM CANDY of choice: Gucci, Prada, Louis Vuitton, Coach, Kate Spade, or some other? No matter which you've chosen, your handbag is an iconic expression of your individuality and femininity. What lies inside the handbag is a secret, private world that reflects what is inside the woman it belongs to.

Those who get a glimpse of the contents of our handbags—our private inner sanctums—will see who we are, what is going on in our lives and in our souls, and what is important to us. Handbags represent the emotional baggage we carry around with us every day. Since other people see only the outsides of our handbags, they make judgments about us based on those outer appearances. But what lies inside our bags—facets of our souls and our inner scars—provides much deeper definitions of who we are and what we have been through. Inside, we carry not just our past histories but also secret clues to our present identities and values.

Ask any woman to define an embarrassing moment. She will probably say that, aside from having her skirt or dress get windblown to expose her undergarments, spilling her handbag or having to dump it out in front of airport security is probably in the top ten. By exposing the contents of her handbag—usually an array of empty candy wrappers, receipts, tampons, maybe baby diapers, lip gloss, and other random items—she shares a microcosm of the many hats she wears and things she manages on a daily basis. Such explicit exposure can make her feel uncomfortable and vulnerable.

If you compare women's handbags to one another, you will find that no two are alike. One may be very neat and well organized; another one may be in complete disarray. During my career working with image and styling clients, I have found direct correlations among women's handbags, their respective personality traits, and what is going on inside their minds and/or their worlds. In my nonclinical study and observation of these clients, I have noticed that women with messy handbags tend either to have very creative minds or to be very stressed out, with lives full of disarray and confusion. These women also have a tendency to be going at a hundred miles per hour all of the time. They are often the ones who are feeling overwhelmed, are spread too thin, have multiple projects going on at once, or have difficulty in saying no. How do I know this? The reason is that, at times, I myself have fallen into this category.

On the opposite end of the spectrum are the women with perfectly organized purses; if you looked inside their handbags, you would see that everything is in order, organized, pocketed, and pouched. There are never any empty gum wrappers, receipts, or movie stubs at the bottom of the bags. You know these women! They generally tend to be very polished, put together, and, at the same time, slightly uptight. They may even have mild cases of OCD—OK, maybe not so mild. These women may be professional businesspersons; often they are in sales. However, this strict organization may actually be hiding another area of their which may be completely out of control like her home.

Any way you look at it, our handbags comprise statement pieces of who we are. Handbags come in all shapes, sizes, and materials. They are such a strong metaphor for the personal baggage we all carry that even not carrying a handbag makes a statement. In my opinion, a woman who does not carry a handbag is telling the world that she is a free spirit who wants to travel light without a lot of "baggage." She may also be incredibly adventurous, creative, and laid back. Now, hopefully you are not beginning to feel defensive as you read these generalizations; they just represent what I have personally observed. But think about the women in your life whom you know well. Think about whether or not their handbags are representative of their personalities and/or their lives, and you will see that there is at least some truth to what I've gathered.

This book is meant to serve as a guidebook full of tips and strategies to keep in your emotional and spiritual handbag for when life hands you a shit storm of bad situations or tragedies. My aim is to inspire, teach, and empower you, and I do so partly with metaphors and analogies and partly with affirmations and exercises. The book is also filled with exercises to help you break free from whatever is holding you back. It is designed to give you hope and inspiration during especially dark days.

What lies deep inside our bags is the stuff we are truly made from or the stuff we are hiding from. This book delves deep into the spiritual, emotional, and physical baggage we all are carrying and looks for ways we can free ourselves from whatever emotional negatives have taken hold. Take a minute to think about your handbag, if you use one. Does it represent who you are? Is it large or small? Is it soft and supple or rigid and structured? Is it a neutral color or a vibrant color? Is it made from leather or fabric? Does it have sassy adornments or metal spikes? Why did you choose this handbag over another? What message does your handbag send about who you are? How do the contents of your emotions and life struggles line up with the handbag that you show to the world? Just like our outer appearance, the public does not see our silent inner struggles. By cleaning out our emotional handbags and ridding ourselves of the stuff that no longer serves our inner beings, we can shift from feeling trapped to being empowered.

Introduction

THIS BOOK IS FOR ANYONE who has ever felt like a victim. Maybe you have been through some tough times or faced a difficult diagnosis. I spent most of my life struggling with feeling invisible—like a victim of circumstances or events that were always beyond my control instead of a massively empowered person. I felt as if I did not matter, because I felt that I did not fit into my family, into roles that everyone else thought I should take on, or into the world around me.

The problem with thinking and feeling like an unworthy, invisible misfit is that it leaves you feeling that you are merely surviving and not really thriving, because you are uncomfortable in your own life. You feel like you are suffocating in your own skin. You are getting by, but you are not getting anywhere. You may even feel like a spectator on the sidelines of your own life. This is what I call the "victim mind-set." I had this mindset for most my life. But it's not insurmountable; I'm proof that by changing your perspective, you can conquer whatever circumstances life puts in your path.

As your perspective changes from viewing yourself as a victim of circumstances to seeing that you have the power to choose not only your mindset but how you react to circumstances that come your way, your mind can open up to new and/or different options. This is the first step in creating a life you love. As a result of this new perspective, you can begin living a life that you design and imagine. You will no longer feel that you have to live the life you were dealt or the life that everyone else expects you should be living. Once your perspective and mind-set align with your divine and authentic purpose, you can begin to do your empowering, life-changing work on your own terms. Then your divine purpose, perspective, vision, and life work become aligned, and you may find that your life begins to open up and fall into place. When that happens, your confidence increases, your empowerment shows, and you're transformed from victim to victor!

As a victor instead of a victim, you feel empowered to chart your own course. This shift in your mind-set and feeling of empowerment will gain momentum, and each small success will lead to another and will slowly build. Don't get me wrong; I am not saying that you won't have any more hurdles to jump. What I am suggesting is that when you face a hurdle or speed bump in life with a perspective and mind-set other than those of the victim, you may be able to handle such obstacles a little more easily and feel that you have more options.

The process of changing your perspective may require you to consult with an objective mental healthcare provider or close friend, depending upon the situation you are facing. Being open to seeking out professional help is a crucial step. If you aren't open to getting outside, honest counseling, mentoring, or coaching and putting the advice into action, then don't expect change to occur. Be open to the possibility of an alternative view or a solution that you cannot see because you are too close to a troubling situation. Can you see the tip of your finger if it's touching the tip of your nose? No, but you know your finger is there—you just can't see it. In practical terms, you may, for example, have massive debt and think that your only option is bankruptcy when, in fact, you may have refinancing options that you are not aware of.

Trusted friends and allies can also offer perspective, but here's a word of caution: sometimes friends have their own biases toward situations based upon how they handled or would have handled them. Their solutions may not be the best ones for you. When something doesn't feel right to me, I consult someone else or use my gut instincts. I also use meditation to tap into the divine within. I practice a process of visualization, which will briefly be described later in this book. The most important thing is to be open to possibilities. Sometimes you may not want to hear someone else's advice, and it may be because deep down you know that the person speaks the truth. Sometimes we cannot see the truth for ourselves or it is too painful to look at. Try not to close yourself off or take what seems to be an insult personally if the intention of the advice comes from a place of love, caring, and service to you.

This book is designed to show you how to break through the invisible wall that is keeping you from your greatness. That invisible wall may be a spouse or relative, a friend, a situation, or even your own beliefs. Some of the suggestions and exercises at the end of each chapter may be a little bold for you, but they are designed to help you achieve life-changing results. Whatever it takes, I am here to tell you that true transformation can be done. We will make it happen together!

Part 1 of this book is a memoir of my inner journey. Here you will get a glimpse of my own background and experiences. I will share my successes and failures, give you some insight into my inner dialogue, and describe some tools and skills to muscle through the hard stuff. You will see and understand how getting to the core of who you are, tearing down the emotional and spiritual walls of what's holding you back, and replacing the baggage with new tools and a new perspective can be freeing and empowering. Throughout this book, you will be cleaning out the contents of your metaphorical "handbag", getting rid of what is no longer serving you, replacing the contents one at time, and/or getting a whole new bag and starting over, just as I did in Chapter 6. The inner journey is the most important step toward building a resilient new you and a new life.

Part 2 will take you through the process of rebuilding or replacing your bag altogether. During this section of the book, I will discuss my inner journey as well as outline the steps in this process that have helped me over time. You will be able to identify what parts of you serve you and what parts may need to change, and you will then begin to piece an emotional and spiritual arsenal of empowerment in your new and improved "handbag" in order to become the ultimate version of yourself. I have used these strategies many times and in different circumstances in my own life to help me gain insight and hope when life throws me curveballs and sliders.

Take a moment to consider the following steps for creating a resilient framework for rebuilding your life.

1. Expose the contents.
2. Ease into the unraveling; it's better to go with the wave than against it.
3. Visualize your ultimate bag.
4. Examine and inspect the current contents in terms of what is and isn't working.
5. Design your ideal handbag; make a Plan A, a Plan B, and a Plan C.
6. Piece it all together with resilient materials.
7. Take one stitch at time.
8. Replace the contents one at a time; get advice, and be consistent!
9. Care for your new handbag; read the care instructions.
10. Get ready to get back to living; walk the red carpet.
11. Learn how to handle losing your valuables and other setbacks.
12. Enjoy the silver lining.

If you follow these steps, I can assure you that you will emerge a different person, just as I did. Some steps will be harder than others will; some will require deep soul-searching for answers. You may even need some help from a close, trusted friend or mental-health professional. Make sure you are honest with yourself during this process. Seek objective answers, and listen to your gut. If something does not feel right to you, then it most likely isn't.

Tapping in to your intuition and instincts will ensure the deepest, most powerful outcome for you. If you are not completely honest with yourself, lasting change will not take place, and you will be cheating yourself. As hard as the truth is sometimes, it is best to face it head on and conquer it. Trust me; you will feel empowered.

Part 1

From Conception to Completion: The Evolution of Your Handbag

Life isn't about waiting for the storm to pass.
It's about learning to dance in the rain.

—ANONYMOUS

CHAPTER 1

Exposing the Contents

MAY 21, 2002, CHANGED THE course of my life. It was the day I hit rock bottom. As I was sitting in a windowless college-lecture hall taking my last final exam to complete my first year of chiropractic school, the sound of distant sirens captured my attention. I sat there in a large auditorium style room about 25 rows up contemplating what the sirens could be about and trying to focus on my exam. The sounds were not unusual, because the university was in what I would categorize as an "inner city." It was actually one of the top five crime-infested cities in the state, and so police sirens, ambulances, and gunshots were near-daily occurrences.

As I sat there, my mind drifted to the earlier that morning. I replayed the events in my mind; waking up to my usual 5:30 a.m. alarm. Only this morning my routine was a slightly different. As I laid there next to Will, I was going through my mental checklist. *Today is the day. I have to make sure I get as much as I can into black garbage bags. I can't forget my social security cards and important documents. I can't forget the girls stuff. I can't forget favorite blankets and stuffed animals. Make sure I have everything essential we need in as many garbage bags as I can stuff in my car. Today is the day I'm not coming back. I can't wait for him to leave for work so I can do what I have to do.* I got up and showered as usual, the hot water soothing and cleansing my body and mind. *Dear God, Please keep us safe.* As I got ready, my mind was racing. I must have been overly cordial to Will that morning because he kept asking me if I was ok. "I'm great! I lied. "Looking forward to having this last exam out of the way."

We got the girls up, dressed and ready to go as usual. Our routine was that Will dropped off the girls at the babysitter's house in the morning and I picked them up in the afternoon. I hugged and kissed the girls, and with lunches in hand, Will and the girls were out the door by 6:30 a.m. "See ya later!" I shouted. Will replied, "Yeah, I'll see ya later." I made sure they were gone for about 10 minutes as I gathered my usual stuff for school. *Now, I have to hustle.*

I raced around the apartment with a black trash in one hand while the other hand gathered up anything I thought was important within eyesight. I headed for the girls' room first and began shoving clothes in bag. As each bag filled, I ran it out to my car. I gathered up important papers, toiletries, towels, and more clothes. My hands were shaking. My chest felt tight and it was hard to breathe. *I hope Will didn't forget anything here this morning and turn around or there's going to be hell to pay. God, please keep me safe.* In about 10 minutes, I had gathered everything I thought I absolutely needed and the car was packed. All except for the spots where car seats would go once I got to the babysitter's to pick up the girls in the afternoon.

As I drove away from the apartment I thought, *Dear God, please let this be the right decision and please keep us safe. There's no turning back now. Our safety is at risk.* I thought about fight we had the night before while Will was cleaning his gun collection. I thought about the look in his eyes while he sat there with his antique ivory handled pistol, pointed at a spot on the wall just inches away from me saying, "If you ever leave me, I will kill you and you will never see the girls again." I thought about him pulling the trigger of the empty gun. *No, Amy, enough is enough. Today is the day.* Those words kept replaying in my head over and over that morning. While my head was consumed with the prior evening's events and attempting to stay focused on driving, a loud voice inside my head said, *Amy, turn around and go get the girls NOW before school and take them with you.*

I very rarely ever ignored my gut instinct when it was this loud. Knowing full well that I may be late to my exam, I decided to turn around and go get the girls at day care. It was now 7:00 a.m and I had to be in by 8:00 and had an hour drive with no traffic. I raced into the babysitter's house and said, "I am taking the girls to school with me today. I am done early after my exam and I want to spend the rest of the day with them." The girls were excited and hopped in the car. They had never been to "mommy's school" and were excited to see what that was all about. Once we were in the car, I called my father from the babysitter's driveway. "Dad, I have an emergency. I am leaving Will today and I need you to meet me at school. I have the girls with me and I need to take an exam." Without any further explanation, my father said, "No problem." My father and I hadn't always had the closest relationship but today of all days when I needed him most, he was there for me with no questions asked.

The screeching sirens snapped me back from my thoughts to the exam in front of me. *Oh goodness, how long has my mind been wandering. I have to try and focus on this.* As I sat there taking my exam, trying to answer questions about muscle attachments and innervations, I became aware of the sounds getting louder and louder. I remember thinking, *Is it my imagination, or are they getting closer?* Regardless, I remained unfazed and continued on. A few of my friends who also seemed unaffected by the sounds of the sirens had already finished their exams and left the lecture hall. As I continued filling in the multiple-choice bubbles with my number-two pencil, the sirens became near deafening. *How annoying!* I thought. *This is distracting! I am trying to take this exam—only two more questions.* I took a deep breath and reminded myself, *Focus, Amy, focus.*

Out of the corner of my eye, I noticed one of my close friends re-enter the lecture hall. This was unusual because, per university policy, students were forbidden to reenter the room while classmates were still taking exams. As I glanced up, I noticed her whispering to our professor who was sitting at the front of the large lecture hall. I could see my professor's brow furrow with worry, and, judging by the look of sheer terror on my friend's face as they stared at me, I knew something was wrong. I stared back. I felt a knot in the pit of my stomach, and my hands began to tremble. Their expressions pierced through me, and in their eyes I saw alarm and concern. They both nodded their heads at me as if to say, "You need to come now!"

By now the sirens truly were deafening, and the other students had lost their concentration as well, particularly when they heard the commotion and voices outside. Not caring whether my answers were right or wrong, I quickly filled in the bubbles on my answer key for the last two questions and made my way downstairs to the front of the lecture hall. My professor's facial expression was one of shock and concern, but he spoke no words. I handed him the exam and answer key, and then my friend quietly escorted me out of the room to a scene I will never forget. *Oh shit, Will is here.*

This particular building featured a wall of glass windows facing the street on the first and second floors. Each window measured approximately six feet by eight feet in size, and there were three windows to a wall. When I emerged from my peaceful cocoon of anatomy questions, I was shocked to see, through that glass wall, a chaotic scene involving multiple police cars, police officers running around, and two uniformed men standing—with my father and daughters, ages three and five years old. I will never forget the look on my daughters' faces; they stood there in complete fear of not knowing what was going on but, at the same time, knowing deep down that it had something to do with them and me.

As I approached the girls, they stared at me, looking for answers. In that moment, my heart broke for my daughters. They looked so puzzled and frightened by the unfamiliar and chaotic scene. I did not know what to say or do and didn't have much time to figure it out, so I did what came instinctually. In those few seconds, I thought, *They need reassurance.* So I knelt down to their level, embraced them both at the same time, and calmly said, "It's going to be OK. You are safe here."

I said the only words that came to mind. Deep down, I wasn't sure that I was telling the truth, but I didn't know what else to say or do. My heart felt paralyzed, even though I could feel it pounding, and my palms were sweating. I looked up at my father and nodded. One of the police officers approached me and asked me to come with him. "Girls, stay here with Grandpa. It's OK; I will be right back."

As I turned to go with the police officer, my younger daughter ran after me and yelled out, "Mommyyyyyy!" She ran toward me, and I gave her another hug.

"I love you…Stay with Grandpa and Sissy. It's OK. You are safe here. Mommy will be back. I promise." All I kept thinking was, *God, please let my words be true.*

What had been unfolding through the one-inch-thick glass that separated disorder from safety was a police chase that involved the girls' father, who was believed to be armed and dangerous. Will and I were in the midst of a volatile marriage with a main course of abuse and a side of control. Police officers were running on foot, trying to capture him. At that moment, I felt like my life was in slow motion, and I was meandering through a chaotic made-for-TV movie. But I was the only one in slow motion, as if I was in an action-movie battle scene in which the hero and villain walk toward each other as if they were the only two people on the battlefield. Only in this case, the villain was nowhere to be seen.

There were police officers on walkie-talkies speaking in code language I could not decipher. Some were running around; others were speaking with students and professors. Police cars with flashing lights were present on all sides of the building. Students were whispering to one another. Professors and staff members were shaking their heads and looking at me. I caught a glimpse of one of the professors looking at my daughters and shaking her head. I felt such deep shame at that moment. I knew that they were all thinking, *Those poor girls. How could she allow this to happen?* I thought, *Is this really happening? Is this really my life? Why did time suddenly slow down?*

As it turned out, Will had been spotted by one of my friends who had finished her exam and left the room. She caught a glimpse of him outside and noticed that he was in disguise; trying to blend in, he was wearing a baseball cap and sunglasses, and he had a backpack slung over his shoulders, which gave the appearance that he was a student at the campus. Upon noticing Will and his strange appearance, she called campus security, who had been alerted a week prior to the fact that we were having marital problems and that I was afraid he would show up at school and cause a scene. Based upon this knowledge and the tip of Will's whereabouts from my friend, the campus security immediately responded and quickly called the city police department.

By now most of my colleagues had finished their exams. Now, along with the university faculty and staff, they were in the building on lockdown while the police secured the scene. I had a feeling that they all could deduce what was going on and that it involved my domestic situation. And by now every person in the building was glued to the glass windows like children in front of a TV. I felt completely mortified that my daughters, friends, professors, and colleagues had to witness this embarrassing scene. Shame and humiliation overcame me, and with every fiber of my being, I wanted to take my girls away and hide somewhere safe.

If there was ever a time in my life when I felt like I had been hit broadside with a two-by-four, this was it. Fear and panic swept over me. My breathing began to speed up, and I felt like I would hyperventilate. With my hand now on my chest, I took a deep, slow breath. My mind was racing with thoughts ranging from *How could I have let this happen?* to *What the hell am I going to do now?*

"I need you to come with me, Ms. Cannatta."

The policeman escorted me down a hallway and around a corner to an area that was isolated from the majority of students, friends, and faculty who were waiting with other officers as the chase continued. The policeman began asking me questions about what was going on between me and Will, our history together, and so on. Quite honestly, I can't remember the specific questions, nor do I remember my answers. I was in shock. The contents of my secret life were now exposed, and I felt so ashamed and humiliated. What was worse was the question gnawing at me: how did I let it get this far?

Blame crept in, and the tears began to flow. I knelt down on the floor, put my face in my hands, and began sobbing inconsolably and uncontrollably. I can't remember how long I cried right there on the floor in front of the police officer. I felt like a complete basket case and a poor excuse for a role model for my daughters.

What I remember most after being questioned by the police that day was this overall feeling of emptiness; I felt that I had become a hollow shell of a person. I remember being talked to but not hearing a word. I was numb. What followed involved navigating a mountain of paperwork, restraining orders, and court motions—all terms I had heard for the first time just two weeks earlier, when I consulted the local women's shelter about creating a safe-exit plan. I remember feeling that my soul had left my body and that I had to make a conscious effort to pull it back into my body in order to pull myself back together.

I know this sounds weird, but when that shift occurred and my mind and body were one again, I could think more clearly and hear what was being said. I remember that once the initial shock subsided, I wanted to make sure my daughters felt safe and reassured. I did not want them to see their mother as a complete basket case, even though I still felt like one on the inside. I remember feeling God's gentle whisper of the word "resilience." *I am teaching them resilience and strength*, I thought.

I was aware that to do so meant something much deeper than merely hiding or masking what was going on with the usual "It's going to be OK" line we have all heard at one time or another. I remember thinking, *No, "resilience" is more than just a noun. This word requires action.* It required me to live with resilience. My daughters needed to see me being strong and not just going through the motions and saying the words. I couldn't just talk the talk; I had to lead by example. Otherwise I would only be setting them up to perpetuate the abuse cycle when they get older. In contrast, setting a powerful example with strong boundaries would be the first step toward giving my daughters any chance of breaking this cycle. Going backward was not an option. I had to move forward and see this through.

By shifting my thoughts away from blame, embarrassment, and shame to those of courage, resilience, and strength, I felt empowered. I could choose courage to combat the shame that I felt. I could conquer the dark feeling of fear and humiliation by shining the light of empowerment and resilience. Like a trampoline that springs back effortlessly after being jumped on, I could spring back. Yep, I would be a trampoline; that would be my metaphor for survival.

Over time, Will would repeatedly try to jump on my trampoline. Those "jumps" would consist of manipulative tactics in the courthouse, slander, retaliatory incidents, stalking, and intimidation. I would often find my windshield smashed, my car keyed, or my tires slashed, among other attempts to derail my future and my daughters' futures. But an interesting internal shift happened after each of Will's attempts to weigh me down: Each jump fueled my internal flame of resilience. As it became increasingly fanned, it grew from a small flame into a raging fire. With each incident, I became more determined to break free from the dark tentacles of shame and abuse. The more I was bounced on, the more I just sprang back, and the fire inside me grew.

I decided that the best comeback would be not only to come out of this a "survivor" but also to conquer this like a hero in battle. I made a commitment, to myself and my daughters, to reach the highest imaginable degree of achievement, and, once I attained that, I would give back. I had something to prove to myself. I had something to prove to my family and my daughters. I had an example to set, and I was going to do it with valor and grace.

As a result of that incident on May 21, 2002, my perspective began to change. In retrospect, I see the incident as a blessing that has made me part of who I am. Now that my deep, hairy secret was exposed, I was free to deal with it instead of hiding *from* it. My new perspective gave me hope. I was no longer a secret victim in my own lonely, solitary world; rather, everyone knew and saw my struggle up close. I felt like a warrior with a new army behind her.

Have you seen the movie or read the book *The Return of the King*, by J. R. R. Tolkien? One scene in the book describes the rightful heir to the throne calling on an invisible army of souls who were held captive to help him defeat the evil Orc army. I felt exactly like the "rightful heir" in that scene. My friends at chiropractic school were the invisible army of souls behind me. I was surprised to have so much support—I thought I would have to face the battle alone. The realization was eye-opening. My internal shift was not just analytical; it was a deeply freeing moment that provided me with a silver lining.

Holding onto a secret takes a tremendous amount of energy. It means telling lies and withholding the truth. I did not realize just how much the act of keeping the secret had drained my spirit. It was my fear of the unknown that kept me hiding and staying in my situation. Once my secret was exposed, help could find me. I suspect that the motivation behind my ex's actions that day was to embarrass me so I would shrink, recoil, and return to what he wanted, where the life we had together was under his control. The opposite happened. My eyes were opened, I became empowered, and my secret became exposed.

AFFIRMATION: I have an army of support behind me in whatever I choose to overcome, and my secrets do not define me. I trust that my army will reveal itself.

Exercise

Think about these questions, and write down the answers.

- Was there a time in your life when you hit rock bottom?
- What did you do to bounce back?
- What valuable lesson did you learn from this experience?
- Is there a big secret you are keeping?
- Do you need to seek outside help with the situation you are facing?
- Who is part of your hidden support army?

In every conceivable manner, the family is the link to our past, the bridge to our future.

—ALEX HALEY

CHAPTER 2

The Past: Evolution of Your Bag

My father is the only son born of Michael Sebastian Cannatta, a Sicilian immigrant, and my grandmother, a full-blooded Connecticut Yankee. I never knew what that meant exactly. "Connecticut Yankee? That's not a nationality," I would say to my grandmother. She would argue with me, and after a while, I just came to accept it. I was always looking for a more glamorous answer from her like English or French, anything but Connecticut Yankee. She held fast to her Connecticut Yankee status. It always sounded to me like something she made up. Little did I know.

It wasn't until I was in my thirties and doing research on Ancestry.com that I found out she was right. She really was a Connecticut Yankee. Her family had lived in Connecticut since the 1700s. My grandmother's name was Henrietta; she was born in 1913 to Harold and Inez Gates. She survived the Great Depression. She became a nurse and married my grandfather when she was twenty-nine—that is, as an "old maid" in her mind. She called my father her "miracle baby," because she gave birth to him at the age of thirty-nine, which was considered quite old by the standards of the 1950s. She had one sister and two brothers. Her brothers were self-taught musicians who played the mandolin and banjo, and performed country and bluegrass music that I fondly remember growing up. She read the Bible every day. Even though she went through periods of time when she did not attend church regularly, my grandmother was deeply spiritual.

My mom is the third daughter of four who were born to Raymond and Pauline Waters. Grandma Waters, as she is referred to, was of Dutch and Swedish ancestry. She was a homemaker. Grandpa Ray was of Native American, African American, and English descent. He enlisted in the army, but he was discharged because of his poor eyesight. He eventually started his own business as an electrician and was quite a successful entrepreneur.

My parents were seventeen and eighteen when I was born. I cannot even imagine what being teenagers with an infant must have been like. Both sets of grandparents were excited about my birth, and so my mom and dad had a lot of support. Grandpa Mike was instrumental in giving me my middle name, which is Maria. This was a "good Italian name," according to my grandpa.

My mom finished high school, graduating second in her class, and my dad went to two years of engineering school before going to work. My mom took care of me with the help of my grandparents, especially Henrietta. My parents didn't have much, but I was the apple of their eye. My mom would make me clothes and Halloween costumes, and my dad worked. Life was pretty good.

When I was four and a half, my brother Peter, the prodigal son, was born, and everything changed for me. You see, my brother was the first grandson on both sides after six granddaughters, including myself. Suffice it say, my brother got tons of attention from both sides of the family. I was really just beginning to embrace the idea of being an only child when my brother was born, but instead there I was, becoming invisible, resentful, and jealous.

I tried all sorts of tactics to get attention, especially my father's. I gave living-room singing performances and threw severe temper tantrums. I tried to be perfect by getting straight As, and I tried acting out, but that only got me disciplined. Nothing worked; everything I tried turned into an epic failure on my part. The only time I would get my father's attention was when I needed to be disciplined—in other words, spanked. From my perspective, this was the beginning of the breakdown of my father-daughter relationship, as you can imagine.

In order to cope with my feelings of loneliness and unworthy invisibility, I played with clothes. I discovered that I *loved* to play dress-up. I became fascinated with all things sparkly and beautiful at an early age, because clothes made me feel beautiful and sparkly on the inside. Even at this young age, I realized that clothes could transform me into other people and take me places. I thought this was so cool: I could transform from being a princess in a castle to being a rock star or a doctor with a just change of clothes. I felt powerful with this knowledge, and I loved how changing clothes made me feel like a different person; I felt prettier and stood taller.

I imagine that this was sort of like acting. Actors pretend to be other characters; they walk differently and talk differently. I was fascinated that clothes made me feel the same way. Not only did I feel confident, radiant, and happy, but I walked and talked differently as well. Fashion had a way of making me feel better and less lonely. Clothes were my quiet companions. Clothes were my vehicles for transforming me to a happier, prettier place where my soul and spirit felt free.

I remember being really excited to begin kindergarten. To me, it meant being out of the house and away from having to entertain my crying baby brother. I had my mother drive by the school before I started. I remember thinking; *I can't wait to meet some new friends.*

My mother tells the story about my first day of kindergarten. Many who grow up in an Italian family think that everyone goes around hugging and kissing one another on the cheek as a formal greeting. This is what I have coined the "Italian handshake." My first day of kindergarten was no different. Before school started, I gave every single kid in my class the Italian handshake. That was the first and last day I did that. I was told I had to tone it down.

Tone it down? I thought. *You people are stifling me! I have things to say and joy to spread!* Toning it down wasn't in my vocabulary. Italians are passionate people by nature. I was not happy about toning it down, but I would try not to go around hugging everyone at school. Toning down my personality made me feel suppressed. Having to suppress and censor my spirit felt unnatural and made me uncomfortable, but it was my fear of getting in trouble that kept my spirit in check. The last thing I wanted was to get into trouble—I was hardwired for trouble avoidance. Blame it on my DNA. What can I say? I was a nurturer and peacemaker at heart with a rebellious side, as you will see later.

Regardless, kindergarten was an awesome experience! I was free from looking after my brother or hearing him cry. I got to color, socialize, and pretty much be myself. Even though I got into trouble for talking too much, I was having fun.

By first grade, I was practically a celebrity. I had already performed twice on stage at school. I sang a solo part in *Parents Are People*, by Marlo Thomas and Harry Belafonte, and I performed the part of Ernie in a Sesame Street skit. I loved being on stage! I felt alive and uplifted in front of people. I was in my element and ready to launch my life. I felt free and easy. Somehow even at that age, I knew I was destined for the stage and for performing. Then came my parents' big announcement: we were moving to the country. I had to change schools and leave my friends. The high I was feeling from being in my element in life changed in a split second with this announcement. Life as I knew it was over.

My fascination with clothes, performing on stage, and speaking, turned to rebellion when I was forced to move in second grade, when I was eight. Rebellion came in the form of dressing like a tomboy, cutting my hair short, and silent withdrawal. I thought someone would notice my heart crying out for attention with this obvious form of rebellion and introversion, but no one noticed the context clues I was giving. *Why isn't anyone noticing my obvious statement?* I would wonder. This left me feeling lost, frustrated, and like no one cared.

My parents decided to build a house on a piece of property my father's parents owned that had been in my grandmother's family for at least two hundred years in a rural town in Connecticut. It was part of a larger parcel with a farm on it. Let me define the term "rural" here. Our idea of television consisted of three channels in black and white, which we only got because of the makeshift antenna my dad made out of tinfoil. If the wind blew too hard, we were down to two channels. I am pretty sure that cable TV was not even available at my dad's house until the mid-1990s. My high-school graduating class was a grand total of seventy-two and was the second smallest in the state at that time. I think the number of farm animals in the town outnumbered the town residents. Did I mention that my house was on a dirt road? To this day, the town has only one blinking traffic light in it.

Now, our house was not any old "normal" house; it was a log home built from a do-it-yourself kit my parents bought. One day, two flatbed semitrailer trucks delivered the logs and supplies to make the house. I watched them unload the pyramid of logs and was fascinated that the pile would someday be our home. By "logs," I mean for-real logs. These were round, hand-peeled logs. Along the length of each one, the tops and bottoms were milled flat with a center groove so that they could stack one on top of another. In between each log, a long spline was placed in the groove to allow for the next log to be stacked in a horizontal, level manner.

"Stand back! Cover your ears!" my father exclaimed. And with two loud booms, the ledge that our house would be built on was blasted into rubble. I had never witnessed dynamite before, and I thought it was the coolest thing I had ever seen. The guys drilled holes in the rock ledge and placed long, red dynamite sticks in each hole.

Once the ledge was blasted, we had to clear the rocks and rock pieces to make room for the backhoes to dig the hole for the foundation. Once the hole was dug, the footers were poured, and we had the foundation for our log home.

Each story of the house took approximately twelve to fifteen rows of logs to complete. Each log was numbered and had to be placed according the plan. It must have been a tedious process for my father, but he loved building things so I think he enjoyed the idea of making a house from scratch with his own two hands. Once the two-story house was assembled, you can imagine how hard it was to hang pictures with the logs being rounded. With not an inch of sheetrock in my room, my four walls were nothing but trees. I was surrounded by logs with no real way of beautifying my space, which was so important to me, because of the rough, rounded walls.

I was in my own version of *Little House on the Prairie*, and I did not like it. I had been happy in my little cul-de-sac neighborhood in a suburban town where I could hang pictures on the smooth walls, ride my bike on the pavement, and be close to shopping and activities. I was happy playing dress-up with my silent, comforting companions. I felt creative in the house on Oakwood Manor. I was happy being known at school. Now I really didn't fit in, not in this house, not on this dirt road, not in my family, and not in this town. I also had no friends, nor did I want to make any. So I became a tomboy living on a farm in a log home. I was miserable.

The house made me feel confined. There was nothing pretty or girly about it. There was no color on the walls, and I couldn't hang posters because the bark from the rough logs would poke holes in them and ruin them. I picked fights at my new school, and anger grew inside me. For whatever reason, no one seemed to notice the fact that I was acting out, or at least no one ever asked why. To make matters worse, both of my parents had to work to support the new house. That created tension and distance between them, and their arguing escalated.

Looking back on it now, I realize that the log house never felt like my home. I couldn't make it my home. With no way to paint, poster, or beautify my space, the house felt like Rapunzel's tower. I felt locked up in a wood fortress. To me, it also represented the beginning of the end of my parents' marriage; ironically the house was built up as my parents' marriage was falling apart.

My saving grace came every afternoon at 3:00 p.m. I would get off the bus and walk about a hundred yards to my grandmother's house to be greeted with milk and cookies. My grandmother's house was the quintessential white New England farmhouse, with black shutters and a wraparound porch. A red barn with a weathervane was positioned about one hundred yards away at the south end of the property. The front door to the house faced the road but was hardly ever used, everyone entered into the kitchen by the door on the side of the house. Walking through this door, the first thing that would hit you was the smell of food. It didn't matter what day it was, there was always something cooking. The delicious smells that came from that kitchen were endless.

The flooring was red linoleum that was made to look like red bricks. About eight feet from the door was a kitchen island with cabinets above it, which separated the inner sanctum of the kitchen from the front door. This separation created a little, open mud-room area. To the right of the door as you walked in was a place to put boots and shoes, and a long oak shelf with pegs for coats. There was also a window on this wall. To the left, against the wall, was an antique china cabinet filled with old papers and some dishes. There was also a doorway to the immediate left, which led into the dining room. The walls in the kitchen and mud room were wallpapered on the top with a 1950s floral pattern. The bottom half of the walls were bead board painted in a deep teal to match the wallpaper. Her house and all of the colors in it were magical and beautiful.

When you stood in the kitchen area, to the right was a stove. As you visually scanned the room from right to left, there was a window with cabinets under it, which created a little seat, and then a corner cabinet with a lazy Susan. The sink was on the far wall, with the refrigerator butted up against it. On the left-hand wall as you faced the sink was a small, round farm table, which was where I would partake of milk and cookies or other assorted sweet confections. The most striking aspect of the kitchen was how colorful it was. My grandmother's dishes were Fiestaware, brightly colored and stacked neatly on the open shelves. The walls were filled with bright hues. It felt warm and cozy.

Every day the first thing my grandmother would ask me before we had our snack together was, "Amy, how was your day?" Looking back now I realize what it meant to me to be valued and listened to. I think she could see the inner struggle on my face. She and I would sit for hours chatting not only about my day but about my life. She invested time in me. She cared and listened. I felt loved. For the first time, I felt appreciated.

In the warmer weather months, my grandmother and I would go for walks outside. She would teach me about the different types of flowers and birds, show how to put mud on bee stings, and demonstrate how to pick apples properly. She loved, cared for, and nurtured me. In the fall, she taught me how to can and freeze vegetables for the winter, and how to make pickles and canned tomatoes. It may be that in these moments spent with my grandmother, my perspective on life began to form. I became more introspective. Growing up on a farm taught me to look for the simple beauty in all things.

My grandmother and I would spend hours going for walks, looking at the clouds in the sky, picking flowers, and studying the microscopic detail of the hairs on a blade of grass. We would look at the grains of pollen in the flowers and sit so quietly we could hear the buzzing of a humming-bird's wings. I never realized how magical all of this was. All of it was fascinating to me and taught me lessons about the importance of noticing intricate details and thinking outside the box.

Life was a lot of work then. We were busy baling hay in the summer and freezing vegetables, raking leaves, and stacking wood for the winter. These were my happiest of days. It was a very simple yet beautiful time spent with my grandmother. Even on the weekends when my parents were fighting, my grandmother's house was my refuge. Despite my rebellious attitude toward farm living, it turned into my greatest sanctuary.

The growing tension between my parents translated into my mom screaming and yelling at my brother and me. If my mom got angry enough, certain dishes turned into Frisbees and wooden spoons became objects of discipline. When my father got home from work, my mother was expected to have dinner hot and immediately on the table. If it was not there precisely at the moment he got home, my father would become enraged. My brother and I were usually told to "go outside and play" or "go upstairs." We would be gone sometimes all day in the eighty acres that surrounded our house. No one thought anything about it. My brother was my shadow, and I remember feeling resentful for always having to entertain him.

Eventually the distance and tension became too much for my mom to handle, and when I was thirteen, my parents got divorced. That was when I realized that Peter was just a little boy and that all we had was each other. You see, after my parents separated, my mother moved out of our house, and I became what felt like invisible to my father yet again. Up until this point in my life, he and I didn't have much interaction unless I was in trouble. My mother's departure hit my father hard. I remember my grandmother referring to my father's withdrawn behavior and saying, "Your father needs your help. He is having a nervous breakdown."

At the time, I had no idea what a nervous breakdown was, but it sounded serious to me. So I stepped up and helped. I cooked dinner, ironed my father's shirts for work, and kept the house clean. I looked after Peter, who was eight.

At thirteen, I felt lost and depressed without my mother around. I had never had a relationship with my father, and I was afraid even to talk to him for fear he would yell at me. I was angry with him and resented all of the chores I had to do on top of looking after Peter. I would cry myself to sleep and would pray to God to deliver me from the pain I felt. I truly wanted to die, and I thought about how I could end my life. My grandmother had taught me that the Bible said that suicide was wrong and that I would go to hell. Hell? I was already living it. I wanted to end my pain.

Despite my desire for God to deliver me from my pain, my inner voice kept telling me that I was destined for great things. I figured that if God had kept me alive this long, then I must have some greater purpose. After all, my parents could have chosen not to have me or could have given me up for adoption. I knew I only had one of two choices: keep living in pain indefinitely or get help.

I was desperate so I decided to reach out to the only person who could help and would listen to me; my grandmother.   I explained to her how deeply hurt I felt and that I couldn't go on living this way. So with my grandmother's help, we went to our local church. At the time, we were active in a small Episcopal church, so we went and talked to the priest, whom I will refer to as Father P. I will be forever grateful for him because I truly believe he helped save my life.

I spent many hours in Father P.'s office over the course of several months pouring my heart out about my problems and issues. He and his wife took me under their wing, and I spent some time with them one summer at their house on Cape Cod—a week away to de-stress and regroup. While I was under their care, one day we went sailing. I remember how I felt in the open sea with the wind on my face. I felt free again, and a glimmer of hope emerged. *I can pull through this*, I thought. *My parents' divorce is not the end of the world.* Well, that's how I felt until I turned sixteen.

None of my pain, nor my new chores since my mom left stopped me from being a high achiever in school. By junior high school, I was a straight A student. By freshman year, I shed the tomboy facade for another façade; the well-put-together glamour girl which felt more aligned with me. All of this was just an attempt to hide my continued feelings of not being good enough, taking care of everyone but myself, and the pain of feeling alone. I became the captain of my high-school volleyball team, vice president of my class, prom queen, and National Honor Society inductee. I also attended Laurel Girls State. I played three sports all year long in high school and was voted best dressed by my peers. From the outside, I looked like I had it all together. I had an abundance of success and friends. Inside, I was crying. My soul felt empty; I was wounded. Despite all of these high-achieving accomplishments, I was hiding deep pain. Keeping up my high-achieving persona made me feel in control. It was my way of not having to face my pain and deal with it. I thought that if I ignored the pain and gave it no attention, it would eventually go away. This theory of ignoring a problem so it would go away worked with the kids at school who bugged me, so why wouldn't it work with deep-seated pain? But the pain didn't go away; it only gnawed at me.

When I was sixteen, my father remarried my mother's best friend and roommate. Let that sink in for a minute. Yes, I said my mom's roommate and best friend. I remember my mother asking her friend if they were seeing each other. I remember asking my father straight out if they were seeing each other. They both denied it until practically the day they announced their engagement. Their relationship appeared to my brother and me as one of secrecy and deception. Peter and I both reacted to their marriage proposal very negatively. My father and our soon-to-be stepmother made efforts to try to talk to us about it, but Peter and I were just too bitter with both of them. When my brother and I tried to discuss the idea of postponing their impending nuptials in order for us to sort out our feelings, our idea seemed to fall on deaf ears. We were told they were getting married no matter what and we just had to deal with it. Their marriage train was in full steam, along with my anger. My pain was building.

After they were married and my stepmother and her two kids from a prior marriage moved in, my relationship with my father took a drastic downhill spiral and completely fell apart. It was completely broken. I had lost all respect for him, as well as the belief that he had ever cared about my feelings or me. I lost hope that he had ever loved me. I lashed out at my stepmother, who became the physical and verbal brunt of my anger. I would swear and yell abusive things to her. She and my father tried to talk to me about my behavior. They would ask me why I was so mad, but it was no use explaining it if they didn't see that their deception and secrecy felt very damaging to me. I felt disrespected, and I felt deceived and lied to about their relationship. I felt that my stepmother betrayed my mother's friendship. So when I was given a letter from my father with a choice to either improve my attitude and behavior toward my stepmother or leave the house, I decided to take my golden ticket and go live with my mother in another town.

Running away from my problems didn't solve anything at the time. What it did was to get me out of a heated, emotionally toxic environment. My father made efforts after that to speak to me, but I chose to keep my distance, protect my feelings, and not engage in conversation. By now, the pain was deep and scars were forming. Deep down, I knew that talking about it would not change anything. I had tried that before. So it was best for me to leave. I missed my everyday interaction with my grandmother and my brother, but it was the price I chose to pay for my own peace of mind.

After graduating high school in the top ten, I was left with a "What's next?" feeling. I had had no college preparation, and I thought my only option was to go to community college or work at McDonald's. My parents did not have the financial resources or the tools to help me figure out what my college options were, and I got the impression that going to college was not that important to either one of them; my mom never went, and my father went for just two years. They got jobs and survived without a college education, and so could I—at least that was my impression.

I was on my own to figure it out. Resigned to the fact that I would not be able to attend a university, I decided that I would start community college and get my business degree. I was unhappy at community college, because I had this feeling in my heart that I was destined for and capable of so much more. I felt disappointed that my parents didn't help me figure it out when all of my friends had gone off to college, and I felt ashamed that I didn't have the same opportunity to go away to college like my friends despite my capabilities. I felt like less than what I was capable of. It was at community college when I met Will.

When I first met Will, I thought that I had met my "knight in shining armor" and my ticket to freedom away from the mundane feeling I was immersed in. Will was charming and very complimentary of me. He listened to me and seemed to understand what I was going through without me having to explain myself. Will was also from a divorced family, and so we had that in common. He was six years older than me, and being with someone older and more mature was appealing to me. Will had two sons from his first marriage, which he said ended because his wife cheated on him. I remember feeling bad for him. He seemed nice and had had his kids taken away by an unfaithful woman.

By the end of my first year of community college, Will had swept me off my feet and convinced me to go live with him in western New York. We had only known each other six months, but it all sounded so romantic at the time. If you have ever been to western New York or you live there now, you know that it is anything but a fairy-tale place. Love is truly blind.

My parents weren't happy about my decision to live with Will, but because I was legally an "adult," they had no choice but to accept my rebellion. Running away from my family and my problems seemed like the best option to take me out of my current set of circumstances. After all, I had been raised to believe that I had three choices in life: get married and have kids, be a nurse, or be a secretary. So I chose the first option because the other two had absolutely no appeal. Little did I know that this was the beginning of a ten-year isolating journey through an insidiously growing world of abuse.

So here are the contents of my handbag so far up to this point in my life; guilt, neglect, lack of self-worth, depression, rebellion, resentment, anger, and betrayal along with a lack of resources mindset. But, there is also self-reliance, beauty, grace, determination, courage, hard-work, and love.

AFFIRMATION: My bag's contents don't define me. I am in control of my actions and my destination. I have unique gifts and talents to offer the world.

Exercise

Think about these questions, and write down the answers.

* What are your unique gifts and talents?
* What lessons did you learn from childhood?
* What details of your life can you think about that have shaped who you are? How can you change them from negative to positive?
* Who loved and nurtured you growing up, and what values did they teach you?
* Think about a few defining moments in your life. How old were you, and what did you learn?
* What or where was your sanctuary?
* Think about when you were four or five years old. What activities made you feel free and easy, like yourself? (These may be part of your reinvention.)

Life begins at the end of your comfort zone.

—Neal Donald Walsch

CHAPTER 3

Don't Shoot the Messenger (Bag)

HAVE YOU EVER BEEN TOLD something you don't want to hear even though deep down you know it's the truth? About three weeks before I decided to leave Will, a friend of mine said to me quite frankly one day, "Amy, I hate to say this, but you are being abused." I had never heard those words before, and my first reaction was, "I am not being abused! How can you say that?"

I had only a singular definition of abuse, which included being punched, kicked, or beaten up. By my definition at the time, I was <u>not</u> being abused because none of those things was happening to me. I did not even remotely consider that I was being abused, because I had no idea that there were and are various signs and forms abuse can take. I had no idea that being pushed, held against a wall, or threatened with a cocked fist fell into the abuse spectrum. Nor did I even consider verbal assaults, financial captivity, and psychological mind games to be abusive. Nor did I consider financial control or having my credit ruined a form of abuse. I merely thought Will's controlling behavior and excessive temper were part of a "normal" anger process.

This behavior was familiar to me. I had felt my father's anger when I did something wrong, and I had watched my father yell at my mother. I had witnessed my father's psychological abuse toward my mother when dinner was not on the table at precisely the right time. My mother had directed her anger and frustration at my brother and me, and I had dodged airborne dinner plates and accepted wooden spoons as the preferred method of discipline. Basically, I had been conditioned to be the object of someone else's emotional and physical rage, and through the glasses of "normal" that I put on to view the world, I saw things from this perspective. All of Will's behaviors felt so normal to me. I used to tell my friends and family that he was like Dr. Jekyll and Mr. Hyde, without realizing that this was a huge red flag.

My perspective of "normal" needed to change. I needed the loving guidance of a friend to show me that my perspective was a little skewed by my past. But more importantly, I had to be open to listen and accept the new parameters and categories of abuse. As you can tell, initially I did not want to hear it. What I thought I knew about domestic violence and abuse was limited to the black-and-white terms of being physically beaten versus not being beaten. Therefore, according to my definition, I was not a victim of domestic abuse. It turned out that I was wrong. What I thought was a black-and-white answer was not the total picture.

The truth is, as Lindsay Fisher so eloquently put it in her book, *The House on Sunset*, "Survivors are cut from the same string: a strong, fully committed, and unwavering devotion to the people who steal our hearts. As we unravel, we calculate how much more we can take. We never have an answer to that question, but we know we'll keep saying one more try. We survivors sacrifice our bodies and our minds, our wallets and our hearts, for the chance to save someone else. They tell us we're not good enough and we believe it. We're too ugly, too fat, too smart, too stupid, too much. Not enough."

After my initial shock at my friend's comment and my rebuttal, I began to self-analyze. I began asking myself and my friend a series of questions: "Am I being abused?" "What classifies abuse?" "What behaviors does the abuser have?" "How am I being abused?" So this same friend and I sought out the answers from a mental-health provider and domestic-violence advocate at the inner-city women's shelter, just a few city blocks from where I was attending chiropractic school.

When I got the answers I didn't want to hear, I was hit with a harsh realization that despite my higher education, upbringing in a small town, and socioeconomic situation, I was being abused and had been abused for years. It was in that moment that I fell into a fetal position and cried and cried until I could not cry anymore. The truth, as they say, hit me like a ton of bricks or a Mack truck. Once I wrapped my head around my newly discovered truth and accepted the reality, I began to look at my past and myself. How did I let this happen? How did I overlook the fact that my handbag had a major flaw? What were/are my own choices, and what role did I play in this? What parts of my character needed to be reexamined so that I not only got out but did not ever repeat this pattern—and not just so that I didn't repeat it, but, more importantly, so that my daughters didn't repeat it either.

Let me clarify that my inner dialogue did not come from a place of self-blame for what happened. My thoughts came from a place of true self-analysis and a place of prevention. I asked myself questions like this one: *What behaviors toward you did you allow that you would no longer find acceptable?* I had to realize that if I felt disrespected or devalued in the future, I could choose to set a boundary not to allow myself to be treated this way by another individual, male or female.

At this point, I could have easily created an internal laundry list of who and what circumstances to blame, pointing fingers at everyone else instead of taking responsibility for allowing people to cross my self-respect boundaries. My parents' divorce, my father's remarriage to my mom's best friend, and my father's past behavior toward me would have been at the top of the list. The problem with making such a list is that blame keeps us from holding ourselves accountable for our own choices and actions. Blame keeps us in a victim mind-set. Blame and shame keep us from looking at the painful parts of ourselves that hide and don't want to be discovered. These emotions hide in the darkness; until we shed light on them and look at them, we will stay stuck. Blame stands in the way of our own empowerment. Once my initial pain subsided and I reexamined myself, I began a slow, steady climb back up from what felt like was rock bottom.

There is a misconception that staying in an abusive relationship for the kids' sake is the right thing to do. I believe that the opposite is true. My opinion is that it sends a silent message to your children that it is OK to be treated in an abusive way and to treat others this way. My opinion is that the only way children have a chance at having a healthy relationship is for the parent to break this pattern by leading by example. Children need to see that it is not OK to behave this way. When they see you stepping up, they will be proud of you for it in the long run.

No matter how you slice it, I was devastated. After the truth sank in, I felt like I had a new label: domestic-violence victim. I have always found labels restrictive and degrading, and I wanted to reject this label with every fiber of my being. But the truth is that I was a victim, but now I am victorious. As I sobbed in the office at the women's shelter, I began to explain my situation to the domestic-violence advocate. I explained how I had rationalized the behavior over the years and tried to fight, fix, and nurture the dysfunction and pain. I had tried to convince myself that things would get better and be different. *Maybe next year will be better,* I would tell myself. *Maybe when we have kids—or maybe when we are more financially sound—things will be better.*

My list of "maybe when's" went on and on, year after year. Guess what—our relationship never got better, even when the "maybe when's" were achieved. As a matter of fact, our relationship got more instead of less tumultuous as time went on. Trust was slowly and insidiously being broken down while suspicion and anger were building up. Actions did not support my ex's words, so I lost my faith in him and his promises that he would be "better next time." The years went by, and the roller coaster of emotional and verbal attacks along with physical threats followed by promises of change continued over and over again.

On my side, I remember hiding little things from my ex, like what I was wearing to work or what I had bought for myself. I hid these things out of fear of his anger. I didn't ever do anything wrong, but I was somehow always made to feel as though I had. Will's insecurity turned into my problem, and shame crept in—shame that I was keeping such small things from my husband, the person I should be able to be most open and honest with. We would argue about silly things like a shirt I wore, because he thought it was too provocative. It got to the point that a turtleneck was somehow too provocative, which would then lead to a lengthy argument about how I must be having an affair. So it was easier to keep secrets. He didn't trust me, and I didn't trust him.

Since I had spent much of my childhood playing dress-up as a form of therapy, being told what to wear, what I could buy for myself, when I could buy it, and how to wear it was in direct opposition to my inner child and my spirit. Clothes made me feel like I could be a different person. Putting on different outfits could help me escape from my present reality. I could be *anyone* I wanted to be in those moments of dress-up. I could pretend. Clothes made me feel more confident, and having my clothing choices forced upon me was in direct opposition to me expressing my divine gifts and passions. Wow, what a revelation! My spirit was being totally controlled on every level! My spirit was being stifled once again. This realization made me feel even more that my life was in complete shambles.

Then, like a warm mantle of soft fur, this overwhelming sense of peace came over me in that room at the women's shelter. I realized that the feeling of spiraling downhill into a black hole had stopped, and I was no longer falling. I was no longer hiding or feeling ashamed and broken. I realized then that all I needed were my daughters and the four walls around me. My life *was* a mess, but I could fix it. I had a major aha moment: I had a clean slate. There would be no more secrets and no more feeling chained down by the secrets I had been keeping about my abuse. There would be no more lies and no more hiding the truth. I finally felt free of my secrets!

Actually, it was the freest I had felt since I was in kindergarten. I could and would start over fresh. I could live my life on my terms now. At this point, my perspective and feelings about my situation completely shifted. I went from feeling overwhelming anguish, pain, and fear to feeling elated at the possibility of my new beginning! I actually became excited for a moment. I knew that if I thought too long about what steps lay ahead and what was needed to rebuild my life, my fears and overwhelm would creep in. They would enter in thoughts like *How the hell am I going to continue school and support my daughters?* and *How the hell am I going to get through the divorce, and how am I going to pay for it?* So instead of lingering on those thoughts, I stayed focused on the positive ones, which were centered on hope and a new beginning. And then, slowly, a smile came over me.

An interesting phenomenon happens when you have been emotionally hurt in some way: walls of emotional and spiritual protection go up around you as a survival mechanism. From my experiences both with my father and with Will, I felt protective of my emotions and feelings. I was so used to hearing that my opinion was "stupid" or "didn't make sense" that I was conditioned over time to keep my guard up constantly. When there were opportunities for me to speak up, or I got up enough courage to open my mouth about how I felt, my feelings were heard but never acted upon. I never seemed to see any signs of respect for my feelings on the part of the person I felt hurt by.

For example, although Will would express a desire to hear how I felt, his behavior never changed. And then, to top it all off, he would pummel me with questions about my feelings, which made me feel either completely stupid for voicing them in the first place or as if my feelings themselves had no basis. So the whole process felt completely futile, and herein was my inner conflict. Naturally, I wanted to close off and protect the inner part of myself (part of the fight-or-flight mechanism), but I knew on some level that I needed to let my guard down and get help.

Letting my guard down was not easy. It made me feel uncomfortable and insecure—two feelings I prefer to avoid at all costs. My DNA is hardwired for avoidance and self-protection, and to me opening up meant that I could be ridiculed or questioned about my feelings. Changing my perspective about opening up and expressing my feelings took trust and work with a therapist. You see, when you have been emotionally or verbally beaten down time after time, have your words used against you, or threatened, you just stop speaking up. You feel like you and your feelings don't matter. Before you know it, you're even afraid to voice an opinion about the simplest things like what's for dinner. You lose yourself and your feelings over time. At least that was my perception and experience.

In the beginning, I had to take baby steps when it came to expressing my feelings. At times, the feelings were too painful to talk about, and all I could do was sit and cry with my therapist. That was OK. It was a start, and, after the tears, I could talk a little bit about my feelings. Over time, I was able to open up more and more as the grip of Will's intimidation, emotional and psychological torture began to lose its hold over me. I had to learn to trust that my feelings would not be attacked. This meant I had to listen to and trust in the therapist's word that I had a safe place to let my guard down. I had to take the advice of people who loved and cared about me for my own good.

In order for you to choose to move forward to get out of whatever situation you are in, you first have to take a risk to reach out for help, allowing yourself to open up and trust. At first, this step is monumental and scary. Your ability to trust what this person has to say is key. Trust that this person has your best interests at heart. Be open—open with your heart, your head, your ears, and your soul. Again, opening up after a long period of having to be emotionally and spiritually protective does not feel natural at first.

Likewise, taking advice and putting it into action is not easy. Sometimes you may even be faced with having to deal with your abuser under the same roof even after you decide to separate. I have heard stories from victims saying that they had to return to their residences so that they wouldn't lose their homes. Abusers may even want to trick their victims into thinking they have changed so the victims will come back. When I decided to leave, and I stood my ground on that decision, Will decided to retaliate. Your experience may be the same. Whoever hurt you may choose to retaliate against your new set of boundaries and mind-set.

Putting up a new set of boundaries is crucial, but it is not easy. I needed help in learning what appropriate normal boundaries were and how to create them. I had to make a list of a firm set of boundaries with a professional. Setting new boundaries in writing was the easy part. Following through and standing your ground is a hold different ball game. It requires sending a consistent message to your abuser when faced with decisions or conflicts. Consistency is key! I learned this when my ideas opposed Will's with regard to custody arrangements. Will, for example, stated in court that he wanted full custody with me having visitation, and I was bound and determined to prevent that from happening. I had to take a very firm and consistent stand on this in order to combat his bullying. I had to detach from the emotional aspect of my mind, which kept saying, *How could he even rationally propose such an absurd request?* I had to become robotic in my answers in court. I had to keep saying over and over, "This is unacceptable." Sometimes this robotic detached approach was difficult to keep up, especially when I could feel some of my past thought patterns would creep in. I cannot stress to you enough how much a consistent, unwavering message helped me during this time. I felt like I was dealing with a child trying to wear me down over a temper tantrum. I remember having to think deliberately about shifting between two opposing mind-sets as if I were flipping an on-and-off switch. When I needed to put up the boundaries, the switch went on like an invisible force field. When I needed help or nurturing, the switch went off, and the invisible shield came down. This was a technique that I developed in an effort to help me visualize the spiritual and emotional wall I required as a boundary. I used it when I felt I needed it.

Letting down my protective shield taught me a lot about vulnerability. I didn't like vulnerability; it felt uncomfortable and awkward. Vulnerability made me feel anxious, and it triggered feelings of being attacked. For me, vulnerability was a trigger to put up a protective shield. I had hidden behind this shield my whole life, and now, did someone say that I had to let my walls down and be vulnerable so I could get help? Well, my protective shield didn't go down without a fight. I was terrified of being hurt. I spent years designing and perfecting those walls, and they had served me well. I had, over the course of my life, managed to hide my feelings behind the walls of high achievement. I had stuffed so much into my handbag that the vulnerability felt as if the contents had been exposed.

I realized that I don't do vulnerability well. As a matter of fact, I don't do vulnerability at all! Vulnerability feels messy and gooey. It is not pretty or sparkly. Vulnerability is not neat and orderly. It is not compartmentalized. No, I don't like feeling vulnerable. Vulnerability to me reminds me of myself as a little girl on the floor throwing a temper tantrum. It wasn't pretty, and I was taught that good girls just "didn't act that way." I hid my pain well, and my protective shield had served me well all these years. On the outside, I looked like a beautiful young woman with everything together, just like my handbag, and that is just how I wanted to keep it.

You see, I grew up in a family in which difficult things or the gooey, messy, raw emotional stuff were never talked about. I was an expert at avoidance and compartmentalizing my feelings and emotions in order to keep them from being messy or spilling over. I found it easy not to be vulnerable or emotional. I could shove my emotional stuff under the proverbial rug, and I thought that if it was out of sight, it was out of mind; eventually the raw emotion would just go away. Do you also have a giant pile of emotional baggage under your rug? Why shove it under the rug when there is a perfectly good handbag to shove it in? By now, mine was bursting at the seams.

AFFIRMATION: I am taking consistent steps toward my future by allowing trust to enter my being.

AFFIRMATION: I am choosing to shed light on shame and blame, and to replace them with resilience and courage.

Exercise

Think about these questions, and write down the answers.

- What situation in your life do you need help with?
- Do you have people in your life trying to tell you something, but you just don't want to hear what they have to say?
- What protective mechanisms do you have, and how do they affect your perspective of the situation?
- What actions can you take to examine your protective walls so that you can let them down and move forward?
- What emotional baggage do have you shoved in your bag?

Here are a few signs that it's time to get help. Please seek a mental-health professional if you answer "yes" to any of the following questions.

Signs That You're in an Abusive Relationship	
Your Inner Thoughts and Feelings	**Your Partner's Belittling Behavior**
Do you... feel afraid of your partner much of the time?	**Does your partner...** humiliate or yell at you?
avoid certain topics out of fear of angering your partner?	criticize you and put you down?
feel that you can't do anything right for your partner?	treat you so badly that you're embarrassed for your friends or family to see the interaction?
believe that you deserve to be hurt or mistreated?	ignore or put down your opinions or accomplishments?
wonder if you're the one who is crazy?	blame you for his or her own abusive behavior?
feel emotionally numb or helpless?	see you as property or a sex object, rather than as a person?

Your Partner's Violent Behavior or Threats	Your Partner's Controlling Behavior
Does your partner... have a bad and unpredictable temper?	**Does your partner...** act excessively jealous and possessive?
hurt you or threaten to hurt or kill you?	interrogate you about where you go or what you do?
threaten to take your children away or harm them?	keep you from seeing your friends or family?
threaten to commit suicide if you leave?	limit your access to money, phones, or the car?
force you to have sex?	tell you who you can or cannot speak to?
destroy your belongings?	constantly check up on you?

Take a walk in my shoes before you judge me.

—Anonymous

CHAPTER 4

The Stitches Became Unraveled

THE TWO AND A HALF years that followed the May 21, 2002, incident were not any easier. That day was the only the beginning of a series of battles in a long war over custody, finances, and my freedom. Many highs and lows and wins and losses were still to come.   During this time, I became completely unraveled. If you have ever been abused or known someone who has been emotionally, psychologically, or physically abused, then you know about the roller-coaster cycle. After a violent or abusive episode, the abuser often tries to make amends, apologize, or convince the abused person that he or she has changed. Many times, the abuser will also use some other tactic of guilt or manipulation, such as buying flowers, persuading the abused that he or she overreacted, or making an attempt to reconcile, with the objective of regaining control over the abused. My situation was no exception to this pattern.

I won't get into all of the details of the next two and a half years, but suffice it to say that whenever I stood my ground and conveyed the clear and consistent message that I was not coming back, even for "the girls' sake" (as he put it), some form of retaliation would occur, usually in an up-and-down pattern. First, there would be a period of Will's "playing nice" to try to manipulate me, followed by me standing my ground, followed by another retaliation. This went on and on. Dealing with these events was exhausting and distracting. Retaliations came in the form of smashing my windshield, keying my car, and slashing my tires in addition to custody battles and even my own arrest.

Now, growing up on a rural farm in Connecticut did not prepare me for police, courts, and restraining orders. I lived a simple, quiet, hard-working existence, peacefully doing my own thing. I had never heard the term "restraining order," nor did I even know what one was before that period of my life. But what <u>did</u> prepare me were the values my grandmother taught me, which were resilience, patience, and persistence; each of which were solid parts of my handbag.

So, you may be wondering, how does the victim of domestic violence come to get herself arrested? Well, I will tell you. During the process of the custody battles and divorce, the court determined that it would be best for the visitation exchanges be done inside the local police barracks with police witnesses present, due to our volatile history. (You also may be wondering how in the world my ex got joint-custody visitation rights with all that transpired. That is another story.)

One day while exchanging the girls and their belongings with Will at the local state police barracks, he approached me and verbally assaulted me as I got out of my car. For fear that he would damage my vehicle, newly fixed from the latest act of vandalism, I yelled at him, "Get away from my car!" As he continued to approach me, I felt my chest tighten with fear and yelled, "Get the f*** away from me!"

Now, I know it wasn't very ladylike for a small-town country girl to yell obscenities, but I couldn't help it. Maybe it was the false sense of safety of being at the police barracks that made me feel empowered to swear at him and stand up to him for the first time in years. Maybe it was temporary insanity that met his verbal assault and physical posturing with resistance. I am not sure. Either way, I was not going to let Will bully me anymore. As he continued to approach me, firing off verbal accusations and telling me what a horrible mother I was and that I couldn't fool everyone, with my heart pounding and my chest tightening I placed two hands on his chest and, with one last "Get the f*** away from me," shoved him out of my way. He stumbled back about two feet but never lost his foothold. With a smirk on his face that I will never forget, one that seemed to say, "I'll show you," he quietly turned around and marched into the barracks as if he were a proud, spiteful winner.

I had no idea what was coming next, but let me tell you that what happened was the furthest thing from my mind. In the midst of feeling proud of myself for finally standing up to him for the first time in ten years, I saw two state police troopers emerge from the front door of the barracks and approach me, saying, "Ms. Cannatta, you're under arrest for assault."

"What? Me? What did I do?"

In that moment, all the pride and strength I had was drained instantly from my body. Anyone who saw my face at that moment would have said that I looked ghost white. Wait a minute! This man, who has caused me physical, emotional, and verbal harm for years, is pressing charges against me? I had had plenty of opportunities to press charges against him over the years, but I didn't do so, out of fear. Now suddenly he was having me— me, of all people, someone who has never hurt a fly—arrested?

"Officer, are you kidding me? And in front of my daughters?"

"Please come inside with us, Ms. Cannatta." The officer said, coldly.

So I went inside, crying my eyes out. *Where is the justice in this world?* I wondered. *How can this be happening? Now he will be even more brazen in hurting me. After all he has done to me, and I get arrested?* I had to give a statement as to what happened, which I could barely choke out after sobbing through having my fingerprints taken. My mug shot looked like I had been stung by bees on my face, as my eyes were nearly swollen shut from crying. *Fingerprinted? Mug shots?* I was a country girl from a rural town. I was not a rebel without a cause. How could this be happening?

I poured out my entire life story to the trooper, including all of the police reports I filed for the mysterious tire-slashing, windshield-smashing, and car-keying episodes in multiple towns, as well as the incident at the college. After that was over, the trooper looked at me and, in a condescending tone, said, "I am sorry, but we see this happen all the time, unfortunately. We have a job to do, which is to uphold the law, and it is not always on the side of the victim."

What went through my mind at that point was something like, *No shit, Sherlock.* But I was obviously not in a position to express that one out loud. So instead, I calmly and eloquently asked, "What are we supposed to do? Allow ourselves to get beaten up and not defend ourselves?"

His response surprised me. "Well, in domestics"—short for domestic-violence episodes—"we have to arrest both parties no matter what because it takes two to fight. You run the risk of getting arrested, but it is always better to call us."

I could feel the blood surging through my body at that point. My anger at the injustice of this statement made my skin crawl and my blood boil. "Well, it only takes one to get the shit beat out of you or killed. This system is messed up."

Without acknowledging my statement, the officer coldly stated, "Ms. Cannatta, you are free to go. Make sure you appear at your court date."

Free? Free? I am not free, I thought. *I am a prisoner in my own life, always looking over my shoulder.* My anger kept on building up inside me. Would I ever be free again?

Even as I write this, my body can still feel the emotions, chest tightness, and adrenaline surge all over again, like it happened yesterday. Now, I am not recommending that anyone do what I did, which was to react without thought for the consequences. Actually, I never thought in a million years that I would end up being fingerprinted and having my mug shot taken. It was humiliating. What I would recommend in dealing with a situation like this is to be armed with knowledge. The more knowledge you have of the process and the legal system, the better off you will be.

If I had known what my ex's motive was, then, instead of giving him a swift shove, I would have quietly marched into the police barracks and avoided the whole scene. As empowering as it was to shove him out of the way at the time, the consequences of my adrenaline rush and unclear thinking are not ones I ever want to relive. I could have made a choice in this situation. I could have walked into the barracks and explained what was happening in the parking lot. Maybe it would have turned out differently.

The takeaway message in telling you this story is that sometimes you have to look your fears in the face—dead in the eye, that is—and stand your ground. It isn't easy. Sometimes this involves facing a boss to tell him or her that you quit or telling a family member that you don't appreciate how he or she treats you. Sometimes facing your fear is taking that first step toward eating healthier or exercising. Whatever the situation is, there is so much bravery in looking fear dead in the eye and conquering it. Fear is merely a speed bump in the road to our success, and we can drive over it! Bravery does not come from doing something you are already comfortable with. It comes from doing something that takes you out of your comfort zone into a place of empowerment.

While I was growing up, I learned that my choices in life were a direct reflection of me and my character. Having this perspective over time put a lot of pressure on me. I felt that I should never make a mistake. What if I made a bad or a wrong choice? Doing so would leave me feeling bad about myself. Shame would creep in, which would lead to depression. Getting my self-worth from this perspective, that my choices were either good or bad, meant that I was either, good or bad, one or the other. When I made bad choices, I felt shame and had a very self-destructive thought process. I think this is why I had so much shame that I was with an abusive person. I felt bad about myself and ashamed. My closest friends would tell me that my choices were not a direct reflection of who I was as a person, but inside I did not believe them. The person in the mirror told me otherwise. It was not until I separated my shame from my self-worth that I began to see that what they were saying about me was true. Reading Brené Brown's book *Daring Greatly* also helped me to solidify the understanding between shame and self-worth.

One of the most common questions I get asked when I share my story is, "Why didn't you press charges?" Other common question I get is, "Why didn't you just leave?" These are easy questions to ask if you have never been in an abusive situation, but they are hard to answer when you have been. So let me just explain what went on inside my head when I was faced with whether to press charges or not and whether to leave or not. The answers to both questions are the same. The truth is that when you are faced with the decision of whether to press charges against your abuser and run the risk of being killed for doing so, the decision to not press charges wins every time. Until you reach your limit and are ready to make that final once-and-for-all break, you don't dare press charges for fear of the retaliation that will follow. These are the consequences, and the abuser knows this. The problem with not pressing charges when you have the opportunity to do so is that you end up having nothing to substantiate your accusations. This creates a "your word against theirs" phenomenon.

If you are fighting for custody of your children with no evidence to substantiate what you are saying, you may end up having to share joint custody with your abuser, which becomes a complete slap in the face, which is what happened in my case. If you press charges, you run the risk of retaliation or worse. If you don't, then you run the risk of having to share custody. Herein lies the catch-22.

The first thing that went through my mind was, "What will happen if I press charges, and what are the consequences to me?" Sometimes both the abused and the abuser get arrested, and I had been told by police officers that "it takes two to fight." In many instances, if the abuser gets arrested, he or she usually gets out of jail the same day on bail with a promise to appear in court. Once the abuser is out with a promise to appear, he or she may have an "I have nothing to lose" mentality. This mind-set on the part of the abuser is a problem for the abused because this is a critical time for the utmost safety. In some fatal incidents, the abuser will then go directly for the abused to retaliate against the act of being arrested. This was my reasoning for not pressing charges when I had the opportunity.

As the one being abused, your first thought is, *What can I do to survive?* Your body and brain naturally go into the primal fight-or-flight mode. The answer usually is not to press charges and rock the boat, creating a potentially fatal situation. In an effort to survive "one more day," the abused person instead will often attempt to smooth over the situation in an effort to diffuse its intensity. So the abused becomes the enabling peacemaker just to survive. From experience, I have found that this only further perpetuates the pattern, because the abuser believes that he or she has gotten away with the abuse.

Other questions asked of me are, "Were there any early signs?" or "Was he like this when you met?" The answer is no. You see, in the beginning of any relationship, both parties are on their best behavior. People who are falling in love do their best to hide their flaws. Hiding flaws can go on for months or even years, and so in an abusive situation, an insidious onset happens over time. What I mean is the abuse could start one day when the abuser has had a bad day or is in a bad mood. He or she may call you stupid or get really angry, and at the time you think to yourself, *Well, maybe he or she overacted because he or she had a bad day.* So you don't think anything of it; you brush it off and second-guess yourself. Then the abuser becomes crafty at making you second-guess yourself the next time something happens, such as when he or she has another bad day and gets angry. Again, it's no big deal. We all get angry, right? *It's just a tough time right now*, you think to yourself.

This goes on for months and then gradually for years. Then the angry bad days get more frequent, and control begins to surface, such as control over what you wear. Again, this starts gradually through subtle "suggestions" at first. When you question a "suggestion," your partner gets defensive and responds with, "Well, it was just a suggestion!" In that moment, this may or may not cause a fight. The gradual onset of cancerous abuse begins to creep in like a slowly oozing black tar. Time keeps going by, and each controlling suggestion turns into a mandate with a side of guilt, shame, or bullying. The anger or bad mood turns into all-out yelling and screaming. Maybe you yell back, but most times you just keep quiet because you have learned that yelling only makes him or her angrier. There is no winning the argument. You are always on the losing side.

Throwing around words and verbal attacks turns into throwing objects or punching walls. Throwing objects turns into throwing punches, pushing, or shoving. By now, you are years into a relationship. Maybe you are married or perhaps you have kids, and you feel that there is no turning back. Maybe you feel that you just have to live with it.

By now, you have either begun to realize that this is not healthy, or you haven't. Maybe you think, as I did, that other couples fight and behave this way, and that this is normal. I was never punched in the face or kicked, and I had only considered those specific acts as the definition of abuse. Little did I know.

Sometimes the physical abuse turns more violent. As the violence continues, you know at that point you have to get out, but you aren't sure how. You are afraid that if your abuser finds out that you are even thinking about leaving that you will be hurt or even killed. There isn't a day that goes by that you don't think to yourself, *How am I going to get out of this situation in one piece?* If you reach out for help, there is a fear of being found out, and the fear paralyzes you. You get caught between the fear of staying and the fear of leaving—and trust me, it is a place that you don't want to be caught in. This insidious onset of the disease of abuse is now taking over your body and your life. How can you heal and rid yourself of this sticky black tar?

I am big on analogies. I like to think of the abuse-process dynamic like the dynamic of the process of gaining weight. This is not to belittle or simplify the topic, but rather to put it in terms that readers may be able to relate to. Imagine gaining weight at a rate of a pound per year. At the end of year, you would think to yourself, *Hey, not bad! I only gained a pound this year.* But imagine doing that for ten years in a row. By the end of ten years, you would have gained ten pounds. Then you would notice and say, *Wow, I really need to lose ten pounds.* The same thing happens with abuse. You wake up one day and say to yourself, *Wow, this is bad, and I can't take it anymore.* You reach your breaking point.

Now, everyone has a different breaking point or rock bottom. I have heard that this is also true of addiction. No one can force you to stop an addiction, and no one can force you to leave your abuser. Only you can make that decision. It's only when you are at your personal rock bottom and enough is enough that you can make the decision to begin the steps necessary to change. The most important thing is that when you decide to, do it as safely as possible. Consult a professional, and get help. Make a

Plan A and have all of your ducks in row. Then make a Plan B and a Plan C. Have all of your bases covered. It is critical to your success and your safety. After that, do not look back under any circumstances. Keep going, and stay the course.

Think about your own personal breaking point. Do you look back on it and think about what you learned? Do you have unresolved regrets about how you handled the situation?

AFFIMATION: I am brave, strong, and bold. Fear has no power over me. I am ready to take my life back and make a change. I choose me!

Exercise

Think about these questions, and write down the answers.

- What specific knowledge do you need to acquire to conquer your present situation?
- What tools do you have to look fear in the face?
- What strategies can you use to overcome your fear?
- What is your Plan A? What are the pros and cons of this plan?
- What is your Plan B? What are the pros and cons of this plan?
- Are there any other options for handling your situation?
- Are you prepared for the unexpected?

The fact is that it is hard to walk in a single woman's shoes. That's why we need really special ones now and then to make the walk more fun.

—CARRIE BRADSHAW, SEX IN THE CITY

CHAPTER 5
Prada or Nada?

WHAT WOULD YOU DO IF suddenly had to give up everything you had for the opportunity to start over? Would you take the risk? I had everything and then I had nothing. One day I had all of these material things, I had gotten remarried to doctor, had a big house near the beach, a new car, and a new life, but I was a still a prisoner. I had abundance all around me yet I felt completely empty. Then next day, I had nothing, but I had gained my freedom and felt rich.

After graduating Chiropractic College in 2005 with honors, I got re-married in late 2006 to someone who ended up being to a lesser degree, controlling and abusive so by early 2007, I was miserable and began the separation and divorce process once again. This time, I wasn't wasting years of my life trying to "make it work" I just decided to get out quickly before too much damage was done. And so, I started over, again. I just chalked the whole experience up to rebounding too quickly and not hav-ing enough confidence in my own abilities to provide for my daughters on my own because I was not receiving child support or alimony of any kind from Will.

Two things I learned from my second marriage and divorce. Never underestimate your power to provide for yourself and your kids if you have them. As the saying goes, where there's a will, there's a way. I also learned that I would rather be by myself than be with the wrong person. So, I decided to raise my standards and wait as long it took to find someone exceptional for me. It's never too late to start over and reinvent yourself.

August 28, 2008, was the day I signed my first lease on my own apartment and the day I opened my chiropractic office, just thirty days after buying my first car. With my own business, my first car, and my first apartment, I was on my way. Holy shit, was I scared! In the two months prior to that, I had been living a nomad –like existence, as a doctor mind you, with family or on friends' couches. I felt like a complete and total loser. Married and divorced twice, with no home, no car, and no income. All I had was my freedom and a piece of paper with the word "doctorate" on it. I felt embarrassed and ashamed every time it was my turn to have the girls for the custody arrangements. I was certain that my worst nightmare of Will taking me back to court to get full custody of the girls would come to pass because we did not have a home. It didn't seem to bother them that we were living this nomadic existence but it really bothered me.

I had worked hard to be a doctor. I spent over four years, forty hours a week, driving an hour and half each way, raising the girls and dealing with all of my custody and divorce proceedings while maintaining a 3.5 average. I overcame incredible odds to gain freedom and independence, but I was scared. I felt excited and exhilarated and, at the same time, afraid to be on my own with my daughters. What if I couldn't make ends meet? What if I ended up on the street? What if I couldn't afford groceries? What if I had to swallow my pride and ask for help? My inner demons were running rampant, and it was time for me shut them up once and for all.

At that moment, I made the decision that, no matter what, I would rather work five jobs than ask my ex for financial support of any kind. I also knew that if I did, he would hold it over my head. I didn't want to ask him for anything, because that meant a fight I was not up for. The cons outweighed the pros on this one. I knew he would never just do the right thing in the best interests of the girls, especially if it meant getting even with me or making my life more difficult. I had learned this lesson during our divorce.

Our two-and-a-half-year court battle resulted in me selling my last reminder and remainder of my grandmother, which was a parcel of family property she had left me, in order to pay Will his half of my assets and pay $25,000 in legal bills from the custody and divorce proceedings. I ended up with nothing. Giving up that piece of her was one of the hardest obstacles I had to overcome, but I didn't see any choice at the time. My attitude was that I could do this on my own. I had a fledgling practice, was working full-time in retail management at Kate Spade, and was also working overnight one night a month at J. Crew. I thought I should have been able to make a great living and not have to worry about anything.

Our first apartment was a second-floor apartment overlooking the Connecticut River. It was beautiful, with an open floor plan, two bedrooms, and a bathroom. There was a deck off the master bedroom just large enough for a small table with chairs and a grill. We were within walking distance to a marina, a market, an ice-cream shop, and a boutique store. We had neighbors! It felt safe. It was perfect for the three of us. This was our place, a safe place for just the three of us. It was a blank white canvas waiting for us to make it our home, and that's just what we did.

Our first meal at 38 North Main was fried chicken and potato salad made by my mom. We ate sitting on the floor around a cardboard box we used as a table. The girls to this day still remember how special that first meal was. It didn't matter to them that we had no furniture or that we were sleeping on pool floaties and air mattresses I had borrowed from family. It didn't matter that we had paper plates and plastic utensils. We had one another, and they knew they could count on me. That dinner was magical. We felt happy and safe for the first time. We didn't have anything but our clothes and air mattresses, but it didn't matter. There was a sense of peace for the first time while we ate—the peace that comes after you've been holding your breath and can finally exhale. Fried chicken never tasted so good.

Little by little, we made those one thousand square feet a home. The first thing I did was paint the girls' room sage green. They loved that color. We got bunk beds and new bedding for each of them. We decorated their room just how they wanted. It was their safe sanctuary.

Once their room was exactly the way they wanted it—within what my budget would allow—I began adding furniture to the large, open living area and my bedroom. I started little by little. First, I added curtains so we had privacy in every room. I bought secondhand furniture, which I re-painted or repurposed. The thriftiness and outside-the-box thinking my grandmother had taught me came in handy. My mom lent me have a couch that she bought for sixty dollars at Goodwill. I covered it with an ivory duck-cloth cover and bought new pillows, and we were all set. I was on a roll. I was having fun making all of my own choices and decisions about every purchase I made or added to our space. I remember my excitement when I picked out and bought my own dishes and silverware for the first time. I could get anything I wanted within my budget, and it felt great! I know that dishes and silverware are small things, but they were big to me. I was so grateful for every little thing I got for our home.

When Christmas came that year, I was so excited. The girls and I had complete control over our tree decorations. This was empowering! Ever since I was four, I had a fascination with the quiet, illuminated presence of—the magic—of Christmas trees. Their radiance and sparkle mesmerized me, and I was completely captivated by their beauty. The thought that I had a blank evergreen slate to call my own for the first time was exciting to me. I was so elated to design my own version of sparkly, evergreen perfection that I felt like the proverbial kid in a candy store with my mouth watering, giddy with excitement. No one was telling me what color ornaments to buy or what was acceptable or not acceptable to put on the tree. No one was there to dictate whether we could have colored or white lights. No one was there telling me I had to have a star instead of an angel on top. I could have whatever my heart desired. I finally had creative freedom! I still get excited thinking about our first Christmas tree. We were free to decorate and beautify it in our own way. Funny how something so simple could give us such excitement and pleasure.

The girls and I decided to have a family meeting to discuss the decorating strategy and theme for the tree. We wanted it to be spectacular and breathtaking. It only took us about ten seconds to come to a unanimous decision on the color scheme for the decorations and ornaments for our tree: Pink! We decided to create a preppy, girly tree. We were ecstatic! We immediately got in the car and went to Walmart, where we got every box of pink ornaments we could find! We decided that gold would be a nice accent color, so we bought some gold ornaments to fill in the gaps. We even bought three pink shoe ornaments! When we came home, we went right to work decorating and listening to Christmas carols. We put white lights on the tree and a gold angel on top. When we were finished, we stepped back to admire our creation. I hugged the girls, and my tears welled up inside. We were happy.

As I stared at our pink-and-gold glowing creation, I realized that our Christmas tree was a symbol of our freedom: freedom to choose whatever we wanted, freedom to create life on our own terms. It felt like I was ordering off a menu that I had personally created with all of my favorite dishes on it. My transformation was just beginning, and the girls were by my side. I could tell that they sensed it, too. Their transformations and mine were intertwined, and we had arrived! There weren't many presents under the tree that year, but it didn't matter. The gift we gave ourselves was abundant. I gave them the most invaluable gift a mother could: freedom.

When you think about your own life, do you have your freedom? Are you being weighed down by material things or bills that are keeping you from being truly fulfilled? Do you have an abundance of stuff but still feel empty inside?

AFFIRMATION: I am enough. I have enough. I choose freedom over the bondage of my situation.

Exercise

Think about these questions, and write down the answers.

* Is having expensive, luxurious stuff that comes with an emotional, mental, or spiritual price tag versus your freedom worth it?
* What is it costing you or your children to stay where you are and not to step out?
* What messages are your choices sending to your family or your children?
* Are your choices keeping you from feeling free? At what cost are you willing to sacrifice your freedom?

Sometimes it's the smallest decisions that can change your life forever.

—KERI RUSSELL

CHAPTER 6

Choosing the Bag That's Right for You

WHAT IS THE ONE HANDBAG that really gets you excited when you see it? That one, maybe you own it or you long to have it someday. Is it a Hermes or a Louis Vuitton? Close your eyes and visualize it. How does it make you feel? If you don't own it, how would you feel if you did? Accomplished? Successful? Powerful?

The first time I ever splurged on what I would consider a luxury-brand handbag was when I was thirty-seven. I remember talking to a friend about handbag brands, and she mentioned Coach, Louis Vuitton, Burberry, and Kate Spade. I had no clue what she was talking about. What the hell was a Louis Vuitton? Because I had lived with an abusive husband who didn't allow me to spend money on myself, those luxury brands had eluded my fashion knowledge, even though I did consider myself a fashionista. Once I became familiar with them, they still impressed me as costing more money than I had ever thought of spending on a handbag. I grew up on a farm, after all. I hadn't yet developed my abundance thinking mindset.

One day, my friend Maria walked my through the ins and outs of each of the brands: the quality, manufacturing, and materials. She taught me about each brand's philosophy, demographic, and marketing tactics. We browsed the websites thoroughly. I was amazed that there was so much to learn about luxury-brand handbags. After two hours online, I knew some of the ins and outs of the brands and how to tell a knockoff from the real deal. I spent that day learning about zipper pulls, lining fabric, and of all things, purse feet! Who knew purses had feet?

One thing about my personality and style philosophy is that I prefer quality over quantity. I would rather have one really awesome quality piece than a ton of items that may fall apart after a short time. I also analyze every detail of my high-ticket purchases before I buy. My perspective and philosophy also hold true for buying a car or anything else. My analysis includes where an item is made along with the life story of the owner of the company, the company's mission, how easy the product is to use, whether the company's mission is in line with my values, whether the company supports philanthropic causes or people, and the quality of the raw materials. Does the brand represent everything I personally hold dear? If the answer is no, then I don't buy it.

There was only one brand that emerged that day, after all of my analysis: Kate Spade. I fell in love with this brand and everything about it. How the company was founded by Kate Spade herself fascinated me. I fell in love with her and her story. She made a big business from an idea. She was a visionary just like me. She thought outside the box, something I value. Her company was started back in 1993, when Kate Brosnahan Spade, a former accessories editor at *Mademoiselle*, set out to design the perfect handbag. Debuting with just six silhouettes, she combined sleek, utilitarian shapes and colorful palettes in an entirely new way, and so Kate Spade New York was born.

I also loved the colorful and playful marketing of the brand. I loved the company philosophy of "living colorfully." Coming from the colorless black-and-white world that I felt I had been in for over a decade, my life needed a little color! I also loved her logo. Everything about the brand represented me and the little girl who loved playing dress-up. Yes, this brand is all about me. I loved the brand so much that I got a job as an assistant manager in 2008 and was on the ground breaking of a brand new store locally.

So it will not come as a surprise that prior to the store opening, one weekend my friend Maria and I went shopping at a large outlet mall in

New York. There was a Kate Spade outlet there selling overstock items from the regular retail stores. The little shop was decorated with kelly-green-and-white stripes. The back wall of the store was solid kelly green with the words "kate spade" in white in the middle. Kate Spade never uses capital letters. I liked that. She does that because, as the story goes, she apparently doesn't feel like using the shift key when she types.

As we walked in to the store, I spotted instantly what would be my new bag. It was red leather with gold-plated hardware. Of all the bags in the store, the red was calling my name. Umm, no-brainer: what other color speaks to rebellion and sass better than the color red? I slowly reached for the bag, and my fingertips felt the silkiness and suppleness of the leather. With two hands, I caressed the bag. Yes, it was love at first sight. As I stood there holding the bag with one hand and stroking it with the other in my trancelike state, a voice said, "May I help you?"

"Umm, umm," I stuttered to get the words out. "Can you tell me more about this bag?" The sales associate went over every detail of the bag. She talked about how it could be used as a shoulder bag or worn over the elbow. It was about ten inches long and four inches high. If you looked at it from the side, it was triangular in shape with a long zipper across the top. The shape of it intrigued me. I had never seen a triangular-shaped handbag in red leather. I was hooked already. The strap was attached to the bag by a round gold ring, and there was a circular gold medallion that fastened the leather strap around the gold ring. The medallion was imprinted with an embossed shape of a spade like you would see on a deck of cards. I thought this was the coolest, most extravagant thing I had ever seen. The attention to every detail was amazing. I could appreciate the craftsmanship that went into such a luxurious item.

"I'll take it!" I exclaimed.

The thrill that this bag was going home with me made so excited. I deserved it!

Purchasing this luxurious item made me feel empowered and successful. It was another physical manifestation of getting my life back. *Such a beautiful bag would require a new set of contents*, I thought. I knew that such a bag was impractical when I had groceries to buy. But the little voice inside my head gave me permission. I thought, *Amy, if you keep telling yourself subconsciously that you are not worth a bag like this by denying your desires, you will never have it!* After everything I had been through, having this red bag felt like my reward. I was making a powerful statement. I deserve more, and I am worth more! The beginning of expanding my wealth consciousness was starting to take shape.

During my process of transformation from surviving an abusive situation to thriving, I got as much advice from other people as I could. The advice was great. However, advice is only good if it turns into action. Turning advice into action is up to you. You are the only one who can carry out and follow through with the advice you are given. The ultimate decisions and actions are yours alone. One thing I had to practice and teach myself was to trust my intuition when I was faced with decisions. I learned to ask questions of myself and listen quietly for the answer.

Sometimes there is no right or wrong answer. This realization can be overwhelming and terrifying. Facing difficult decisions and struggles alone can make you feel like you are on an uninhabited island. Depending on your perspective, you may feel overwhelmed. You may feel like there are so many decisions and choices to make that you are not sure where to begin. I suggest tapping into your intuition and prayer along with shifting your perspective from that of overwhelm to that of gratitude. Feel grateful that you have choices, because there are other people in other parts of the world who do not. Isn't it awesome that you have choices? Having those choices is empowering! You have the freedom to choose!

When I began to look at my life this way, with gratitude for the choices I had, my life began to change. My perspective about my life changed. I went from feeling overwhelmed to feeling empowered. I never had the freedom to choose before I made the *choice* to leave my ex. Actually, when I think about it, I never had the freedom to choose ever before! When I began to look at life this way, I felt overjoyed. So many people around the world are living in oppressed areas without the freedom and power to choose. Freedom and choice are the intangibles to be grateful for. When you think about it from this basic level, you begin to see how empowered you truly are. You can also find great comfort in knowing you're on your own. Facing your fears, vulnerabilities, and insecurities on your own and conquering them can be one of the best gifts you can give your spirit. Conquering your life and your insecurities builds a feeling of confidence. When confidence builds, you can begin to feel that you are capable of more and your life will continue to expand.

When you feel like a victim or have a chronic victim mindset, whether it is due to abuse, trauma, or life circumstances, or when you feel like the world or life is out to get you, you don't realize that you have the power to choose. The thought process is that life is against you, and you are powerless to the events around you. This is not true. All it takes is a gentle spark to shift your perspective from feeling like an invisible victim to an empowered being, a.k.a. the victor! When you decide that change is necessary, your mind shifts from being reactionary to being proactive. Every time you don't make a choice for yourself, you are making a choice to remain in a victim mind-set. The active process of making a choice shifts your mind-set from victim to victor and from powerless to empowered. You haven't lost your power—you gave it away freely and innocently, and so did I. You gave it away to someone or something that was unworthy of that gift.

When I came to this harsh reality, I felt angry with myself. How could this have happened? How did I allow this? The truth is that the answers to those questions don't matter. What matters is that now is the time to take back the gift you gave away. Don't beat yourself up over it. Realize what happened, and take back your power!

Self-assessment really takes guts. It is easy to blame other people, situations, or circumstances for where we are in our journey. This is the victim mentality. Pointing fingers only makes you miss the point and is self-defeating. We were given free will by our divine creator. Free will means the power to choose! You can choose to stay in an abusive situation, or you can choose to get out. You can choose to stay at a dead-end job, or you can start your own business. You can choose to disconnect from negative family and friends, or you can keep allowing them to bring you down. Ultimately, the choice is yours.

Wrapping my head around this concept was hard for me. The hardest lesson to grasp is that we also have choices as to how we react when a crummy thing happens to us. Most of us, myself included, want to react emotionally first. Our knee-jerk reaction is to react with blame toward others, ourselves, or life in general. That is a natural human process. However, how much time we spend in the emotions and blame of whatever struggle we are in determines how long we stay in this victim mind-set. How quickly we choose to shift our perspective determines how quickly and productively we can move on.

The pity party begins and ends at the day and time you designate. There is no one else on that time clock but you. And when you decide the party is over, guess what? Your true and closest friends can help you. But as long as you stay at the pity party of one, no one can be invited to help. Your energy is too busy during your emotional state at that point to think logically about how and what you need help with.

For example, when I first left Will, I was so emotional that I didn't even know what I needed help with. My head was unclear. I was overwhelmed and on autopilot. I was in what I would call survival-only mode. When my friends or family asked how they could help or what they could help with, I would say, "Everything." That is how overwhelmed I felt. The problem with saying "everything" is that it is not specific enough for your friends and family. Do you need help with transportation, child care, business strategy, bookkeeping, or something else entirely? When you can center yourself and detach from your emotions long enough to think clearly, you can start a mental or physical checklist of what you need. Once you have your powerful list, you can start asking for help.

Trust me, it is not always easy to ask for help. Some of you may come from a place that asking for help is as painful as having a tooth pulled. I come from a place of independence so asking for help is difficult for me but I have learned there is power in having your efforts compounded with help. Additionally, it is much more fun and the results are quicker when you get help.

What bag is right for the new you? Do you have to buy a whole new one or just replace the contents of your existing bag? Are you ready to splurge on yourself and your future? Raising your vibration and reprogramming your mind to allow for expansion will make you feel more confident and powerful.

AFFIRMATION: I am choosing the mind-set of the victor and not the victim.

AFFIRMATION: I am open to receiving help from others.

Exercises

Now is the time to give yourself plenty of quiet time and space to assess your current situation. Ask yourself:

- What are the most important changes I want to make? What are the most important qualities to me?
- What choices can I make to change my current situation?
- What steps can I take right now to reclaim my power to choose?
- What behavior or people am I allowing to influence me and my decisions?
- How did my choice to listen to those people affect my path in life?
- Who can I ask for help?

Try these other exercises:

- Make a list of things/activities you need help with. Review your list with a friend who can help you find resources.
- For each item on your list, write the name of someone you know who can help you with it. For the ones that don't have a name next to it, have a friend help you reach out to find the appropriate individual to help you.
- Go find your own version of the red bag. Give yourself permission to splurge! Increase your subconscious worth. You will feel different because of it. This will raise your vibration and allow more abundance to flow into your life.

Part 2

Mama's Got a Brand-New Bag

Attitude is the little thing that makes a big difference.

—Winston Churchill

CHAPTER 7

Get Ready for a
Brand New Bag

ARE YOU READY TO MAKE that big change in your life? Then now comes the fun part! So you are at the end of your rope, frustrated with your current situation, and have reached your breaking point—now what do you do? You know that maintaining status quo doesn't work anymore. It feels like just the act of maintaining the status quo will bring on an emotional death of a thousand cuts. Yet you don't know what to do or how to begin to make that necessary change. You have become emotionally paralyzed. Maybe you feel completely overwhelmed; maybe you are scared or feel insecure. You may even feel depressed and confused. Give yourself permission and allow yourself time to feel those things; those feelings are normal! Acknowledge and honor your feelings, but don't linger too long in this emotional state. Doing so will only serve to spiral your mind-set into a vortex of negativity or that pity party that we discussed earlier.

Unfortunately, when you are knee-deep in living your everyday life, it's hard to see beyond day-to-day events or to see your situation from a bird's-eye perspective. But seeing the bigger picture can help you gain clearer insight on whatever it is you are going through. Have you ever heard the expression, "You can't see the forest for the trees?" It has applied to me, and sometimes my friends have had to help me gain perspective of my own forest. Maybe you need similar help. I remember a friend saying to me, "Amy, you're not seeing the big picture!" At the time, I thought,

What the heck is she talking about? Once my friend explained her perspective to me, I was able to step back and see my situation through her eyes. After that, the details about the situation I was in became crystal clear! As a result of my clarity, I was able to make some decisive changes and create a new strategy to move forward.

The sooner you can step back, disconnect, and view the situation from a different perspective, the sooner you will move forward. By "disconnect," I don't mean that you stop feeling. What I mean is, try to stop for a moment, take a deep breath, identify how you are feeling, acknowledge it, and then extract the raw emotion out of the situation or decision-making process to allow yourself enough time to think clearly. It is important to give yourself ample time to process how you feel and then try to disconnect yourself from the raw emotion for a second.

I have found that my own raw emotions have at times caused me to feeling more overwhelmed. What has worked for me is to use this technique of stepping back and separating the emotional "goo" from what is really going on in order to clear the way for conscious decision making. You sometimes have to make a conscious effort and actually tell yourself, "Wait a minute. I am getting all emotional. That is not going to help solve my problem. Let me step back and think about things for a minute."

You want to make real progress, right? That means you have to shift yourself from feeling those emotions toward taking action at some point in time, as if you were a separate being from your emotions. Imagine right now that you a bird flying high over your current situation or set of circumstances. What do you see when you can see the whole picture? What do you feel? How does your perspective change? Now take a deep breath. Give yourself time to think clearly. For every end, there is a beginning. This is your beginning. This is your time. Take quiet time with your thoughts. Reflect. What situation are you trying to change right now? Does it have to do with finances, business, a marriage, or perhaps a relationship?

An amazing thing happens when you realize that you are at the end of your rope. If you can choose at this point to shift your mind toward thinking, *Wow, if I am at my low, the positive side is that I can only go up,* you can begin to feel empowered. If you shift your focus from being in a victim mind-set (*How did this happen to me? I'm such a good person; I don't deserve this!*) toward gratitude for the low as gift, then the healing can begin, and you can begin to move forward. My advice would be not to fight it. Let it go.

There were times in my life when I knew my circumstances were about to crash over me like a ten foot wave and I tried to fight the tide. I tried to nurture my way out of it by trying to smooth things over. Sometimes I tried to get tough and muscle through it. It is human nature to behave this way, after all. None of it worked. It was only when I let go of uncontrollable circumstances, thereby embracing the wave and moving with it instead of against it, that my perspective shifted, and life flowed easier. My mind eased into whatever difficult situation I was facing. Have you ever tried to walk *into* a crashing wave? If the wave is strong enough, you lose your footing and may fall over. But what happens if you walk with the crashing wave? In what way(s) does this feel different? I have learned to see that total destruction in life can be a beautiful gift. Imagine a forest destroyed by fire. You may look at this and think, "Wow, what a disaster. How sad." I look at it as nature's opportunity to rebuild. Seeds burst, and new trees grow. The green begins to return and burst forth from the black char. We don't have to think about it. We don't create it; it just happens. Nature does it all on its own.

Did you know that the oldest living things on the planet are the giant sequoia trees? Did you also know that in order for the seeds of the world's largest trees to germinate, they have to be subjected to fire? Did you know that the bark of these trees is fire resistant and that the trees need fire to survive? Fire actually makes the trees stronger. I love knowing that fact about those massive trees. It has helped me shift my perspective about my own trials by fire. The same holds true for carbon. When it is subjected to massive pressure, it transforms into a beautiful diamond. When I put these facts into perspective for my own life, that has undergone fire and pressure, hope springs up from my soul.

At first, I struggled with shifting my perspective towards that of hope. Thinking that beautiful things and circumstances could arise out of such destruction did not come naturally to me. In fact, I didn't just struggle; I downright fought it tooth and nail. Again, that is human nature; I didn't want to shed the values I had become accustomed to, those which had been reinforced throughout my life. For example, I was taught to stay together for the children's sake and always stand by your man. I felt uneasy with this new mind-set of moving with and embracing the falling apart rather that fighting to keep something that wasn't working at first, but as I evolved and grew, I began to I think about myself as a giant sequoia tree. The more fire I walk through, the stronger I become. This perspective now gives me peace and hope.

The beauty of the pile of ashes or rubble in your life is that you get to be the architect for your rebuilding process. You get to design your life any way you want it. And the fire will make you stronger. Just like carbon under pressure, we can emerge the diamond. When we can replace feelings of devastation with those of empowerment, and can express gratitude for the opportunity to rebuild our lives from the bottom up, real healing can and does happen.

Part 2 of this book focuses on a step-by-step guide to help you transform your life, as well as on some tips to help you not just "get through" tough times but to come through these times transformed into the highest and best version of yourself. Some of these exercises will be difficult and time-consuming. Just remember that you are on a journey; true transformation takes time and is not an overnight event. Some of these steps and tips can be used in a multitude of situations and circumstances. Feel free to tweak and change any of the ideas to suit your unique needs. Give yourself the gift of honesty and patience. Be true to yourself throughout this process so that you can achieve your maximum results.

The following chapters will be dedicated to giving you some tangible tools to help you rebuild your life. My goal is for you to walk away with a new set of strategies and tools in your emotional handbag. Your bag—a variation on a tool kit, really—will be well stocked with exercises and skills to keep you on track for creating your best life possible. We will start out by looking at what to do once you have a clean slate, which is step 4 in the list below. Steps 1 through 3 were covered in part 1 of the book.

Take a moment to consider the following steps for creating a resilient framework for rebuilding your life.

1. Expose the contents.
2. Ease into the unraveling; it's better to go with the wave than against it.
3. Visualize your ultimate bag.
4. Examine and inspect the current contents in terms of what is and isn't working.
5. Design your ideal handbag; make a Plan A, a Plan B, and a Plan C.
6. Piece it all together with resilient materials.
7. Be patient! Take one stitch at a time.
8. Replace the contents one at a time; get advice, and be consistent!
9. Care for your new handbag; read the care instructions.
10. Get ready to get back to living: Walk the red carpet.
11. Learn how to handle losing your valuables and other setbacks.
12. Enjoy the silver lining.

We have all heard that the unexamined life is not worth living,
but consider too that the unlived life isn't worth examining.

—JULIA CAMERON

CHAPTER 8

Examine the Contents Carefully

WAIT JUST A MINUTE! BEFORE you go shoving stuff back into your pro-verbial handbag, let's talk for a bit. Preparing for transition or major life change is not easy. And sometimes life throws unexpected change your way whether you want it to or not. The pieces of your life may or may not be working, whether physically, emotionally, or spiritually. Think about the pieces of your life in terms of the inner workings of a clock with all of its cogs and gears. Sometimes the cogs and gears don't line up. Sometimes one of the teeth is missing. Gears get worn down or stripped over time and need replacing. This is also true of life. Sometimes the pieces in our lives don't fit together or work anymore, and it's time to examine those closely and consciously.

In this book, I use the handbag as a metaphor to represent the emo-tional baggage we carry every day and also as a symbol of an individual's life and identity. Change and transition require us to open up and examine our lives, just as we would open up clocks to fix them or handbags to clean them out. Sometimes the contents of our handbags don't work anymore; we may no longer need or have grown out of particular contents. For ex-ample, kids grow up and we no longer need to carry their pacifiers or dia-pers in our bags. Maybe our shades of lipstick change as we age. Perhaps we have to add eyeglasses. Whatever the case may be, it is important to periodically clean out, add to, replace, and reevaluate what is in our bag. Sometimes we have to dump the bag out and start over.

The process can also require us to examine the emotional baggage attached to the things we carry along. Letting go is one of life's biggest challenges. Whether it is letting go of a dying parent, a child going off to college, or the guilt associated with a past decision, letting go can be emotionally and spiritually transforming with the right perspective. One thing I have learned is that all we have in life is the exact moment we are in. Ask yourself, "How would I spend this moment if it were the last one I had left?" Would you spend it in love or in guilt? Would you let go and forgive, or would you hold on to your resentment? It is important to ask yourself these questions as you examine your identity and the contents of your life. Ask yourself, "What is and isn't working?"

After the birth of my second daughter, I went through a period of postpartum depression. My baby was colicky, and so, for the first seven months of her life, she cried or fussed most of the day and barely slept more than one to two hours at a time. I began using food to comfort myself through the pain and exhaustion. As a result, I gained over fifty pounds and topped out at my maximum weight ever, which was 180 pounds. Now, I know some of you may be thinking that 180 pounds is not that bad. For me, the issue wasn't so much about the weight that I gained as about a representation of how unworthy, lost, unhappy, and miserable I felt. This compounded my depression; and I felt like I was in a downhill spiral that led inevitably into a black hole—I just could not get out.

I was also in an unhappy marriage that was deteriorating in terms of verbal, financial, and emotional abuse. So while friends and family kept telling me how blessed I was and how happy I must have been, the fact was that I didn't want to get out of bed in the morning. Inside, I was crying. There were mornings when I felt like a hundred-pound weight attached me to my bed and an exponential force of gravity kept me lying there wrapped in a blanket of unhappiness and depression. Then one day, I woke up, thought, *enough is enough*, and decided that I had to do something about it.

The sound of my seven-month-old's crying gave me the "wake-up call" I needed. It was my last straw. I came to the realization that my crying, colicky baby was a physical symbol of how I felt on the inside. Something inside slapped me upside the head and snapped me out of my food-exacerbated depression. I said to myself, *Amy, what are you doing? You need to get yourself together!* As I sat feeding my daughter, something else dawned on me. Deep inside me, my perspective had shifted. I thought, *I can continue to sit here month after month being depressed, or I can make a plan and do something about it.*

That day I began taking inventory of my life and my baggage. I made a list of what had to stay and what absolutely had to go, of what was working and what wasn't, including my own mind-set! I listed what I could change and what was out of my control. That's when I got the revelation that the only true thing I had control over were my own thoughts and actions.

So I asked myself, "What is the one thing I can do today to start changing my life and how I feel?"

An interesting phenomenon happened once I decided to take my life back. My baby stopped crying.

What can you do to examine the contents of your bag carefully? Being a leader in your life and of yourself requires mindful and gentle self-analysis. Go easy on yourself. Realize that examining what is working and not working in your life takes time and so does lasting change. Are there areas of yourself that you are truly willing to work on changing? Do you have an open mind? Are there other areas of yourself that are non-negotiable to changing? Think about these areas as you move forward in creating a life you truly desire.

AFFIRMATION: I am taking one step every day toward transforming my life. I am laser-focused toward my goal. I am the only one in control of how I react to each challenge. I can conquer my present circumstances by laying out a step by step plan so I don't feel overwhelmed.

Kick-Butt Exercise

Take a moment to assess your life, and then write the following down, using the worksheet to organize your thoughts, if needed:

- Make a list of the things, thoughts, behaviors, or relationships that **are not** working for your benefit or serving your higher purpose.
- Make a list of the things, thoughts, behaviors, or relationships that **are** supporting you.
- Now evaluate the lists, beginning with the one that is not working. Take that list and make another list of the things, thoughts, behaviors, or relationships that you have the power to change. It's important to be honest here.
- Next, evaluate the list of things, thoughts, behaviors, or relationships that are supporting you. What is the one thing on the list that you can cultivate today? All you need is one.
- Now that you have looked at the two lists, what is the one thing you can remove right now that is not working toward your benefit? Got it? Now go take care of it!
- Do you have the one thing that you can cultivate today? Take time for yourself and go do it!

Worksheet

What is *not* working/serving me?	What *can* I support/cultivate?

What is out of my control right now?	What do I have the power to change today?

What is one toxic thing, thought, behavior, or relationship that I can change today?

_____

_____

What is the one positive thought, relationship, or behavior that I can cultivate today?

_____

_____

If you don't design your own life plan, chances are you'll fall into someone else's plan. And guess what they have planned for you? Not much.

—*Jim Rohn*

CHAPTER 9

Designing and Creating Your Ideal Handbag

Have you ever been so afraid to do something that it keeps you paralyzed? Fear of retaliation is what keeps us in the abusive situation. Retaliation can come in various forms. Often unimaginable things happen such as mysterious acts of stalking, vandalism of personal property, and false accusations, just to name a few. Using courage to combat this fear is the only way out along with being safe. You will reach your tipping point just as I did and decide that it is time to move on. The fear is real but it is keeping you stuck. Breaking free from your fear can be your choice. Your freedom begins with deciding not to let the fear of the unknown keep you from moving forward then making a step-by-step plan, sticking to it, and executing it with help.

Creating a plan is a crucial step in getting out of almost anything, whether it is an abusive relationship, a dead-end job, financial matters, or a difficult family situation. Executing the plan takes courage. Courage requires backing of a support team. Finding a personal support team of objective experts is the key. Start with your closest friends and allies. At times, your friends and allies may not be able to directly help you create and execute your plan but I have found can be a great resource of referrals to get you connected to the people you need to help you with whatever situation you are facing.

After I wrapped my head around the fact that I was in an abusive situation and needed to get out, as you know, I consulted with the counselor at the women's shelter near my chiropractic school with the help of a friend. My friend was not in a position (nor did she have the expertise) to help me create a plan and exit strategy but she found the resources for me and connected me with the experts I needed at the time. This holds true for nearly every challenge in life.

I remember feeling so much anxiety about going to the women's shelter with my friend. I remember thinking, *What if Will is following me and finds out I am here?* This type of feeling can be paralyzing. I remember wanting to go and get help but also part of me *not* wanting to go for help out of fear of being caught but also fear of what they might tell me. It was the fear of the unknown that could have kept me stuck. I could have easily chosen not to take that courageous step toward my freedom. Every time I felt weak, I would visualize my daughters' faces and become stronger.

This leads me to another important point I must mention which is to keep your eye on the prize. A great plan needs to have an end result no matter what you are trying to accomplish. You have to have a Point A and a Point B. Visualize the outcome you wish to have. Not only visualize it, but write it down or cut out pictures. This tells the Universe that you expect the best possible scenario and will help to manifest exactly that. Do not focus on the "what if's", they will only drag you down. Visualize in your mind as clear as you can what you wish your desired outcome to be.

The counselor stressed the importance of making a safe-exit plan. She walked me through the process, which initially felt overwhelming. Once I felt confident that I had a plan in place, I thought I would feel more empowered. Nothing could have been further from the truth. Instead, I felt more terrified, because now I had to figure out how and when to execute the plan. Having the plan was great, but following through was a whole different ball game. The inner what-if demons of fear were at it again: *What if something happens? What if he finds out I am leaving and retaliates? What if the plan fails?* The first thing I remember doing was telling my close friend what my plan was and walking through it with her. We also came up with some alternative plans for those "what if" moments. This helped ease my anxiety.

Creating a plan for the "what if" scenarios may seem to contradict what I said about not focusing on the "what if's" in the previous paragraph so let me clarify. From my experience, preparing for those scenarios helped ease my fears but when it came to the time when I had to execute the plan, I visualized and repeated out loud what I wanted the outcome to be. And guess what happened? The best possible outcome! I didn't even have to concern myself with all of the what-if possible scenarios after all!

Now, I am not a mental-health professional, so I suggest that you seek out help to formulate your own plan when you choose to do so. Every situation is different and requires careful and thoughtful planning as well as timing. This statement is not meant to overwhelm you, but just to point out that in order to be safe and successful, it is best to get help from someone who knows the details of your exact situation so you can take it step by step in manageable pieces. At the end of this chapter, I will share with you some tips that helped me; however, I do not mean for them to replace seeking professional help.

Strategic planning is a valuable life skill that I would highly recommend learning about. I used to think that it was just for business and projects, but I realized that it can help in life too especially during times of emotional stress. I have found that this is because it helps remove us from the situation so we can view it from a more systematic perspective. In a sense, learning this skill is like creating your own handbag from scratch, instead of just replacing the contents. It is a process that can be applied to other situations, like starting a business or leaving a job. The process itself will vary based upon your situation, but the basic structure of the planning process is very similar. Most planning strategies involve an end goal or result, a step-by-step pathway to achievement, and a reasonable time frame in which to reach the goal. If this idea of strategic planning sounds overwhelming and time consuming to you, don't worry. If you need help learning this skill, there are mentors available to you.

If you are in an abusive situation and are not in a position to leave yet, you will need to create code words, signs, or signals to use with trusted friends or relatives to let them know when you are in danger. You will have to come up with a creative way to talk to your friends or relatives about this, let them know what the words are, and indicate what they need to do when they hear you say them or see that you have texted them. This can be tricky if the abuser finds out, and so you will have to be very careful. Make sure to erase your text messages or e-mails immediately, and always clear your trash folder.

Imagine how you will feel when you overcome the fear that is keeping you paralyzed from moving forward in your life in whatever situation you are facing. Maybe you are afraid to approach your boss for a raise, so you don't ask. Maybe you are afraid to talk to someone who hurt you out of fear of their reaction, so you don't speak up. It is the fear that is holding you back from becoming your greatest self, so why not step up, take courage, and overcome so you can hold your head high and feel proud?

AFFIRMATION: I am creating a strategic plan that I feel comfortable with. I am visualizing and speaking my desired outcome over and over.

Exercise

Here are some (just a few, really) tips for making an exit plan from an abusive situation:

* Sit down with a friend or counselor and make a step-by-step plan. Then think of the what-if scenarios and plan for those, too.
* Make sure to have the phone number of your local women's shelter memorized! Do not put it into your phone, because your abuser may go through your phone and retaliate.
* Let someone you trust know what your plan is.
* Set money aside! This may take some careful planning and some time before you leave. Have a friend hold onto it for you. Make sure you have enough to cover your immediate needs for at least one or two months while you get on your feet.
* If you can, keep a journal of the abuse. You may have to keep your journal with a friend or relative prior to your departure.
* If you have kids, make sure that they understand that it is their only (collective) job to stay safe; it is not to protect you. Reassure them that they will be safe. Don't scare them, but teach them what to do in case the abuser kidnaps them or breaks into the house.
* If you have to sneak away, make a plan on how to do so and tell someone once you have done that.
* If you have time, pack a bag. Include everything you will need if you have kids. Make an extra set of keys. Make sure you have important documents such as birth certificates, social security cards, driver's license, marriage license, medical records, insurance cards, and any other paperwork that is important to you.
* Before leaving, and if you have extra time, remove items from the home that you will need that will go unnoticed by your abuser. This could take a few weeks. Things that you will need when you are on your own include towels, maybe extra dishes if you have them, extra clothes for the kids, and so forth. If you have a friend

who can store these items for you, then let her or him do so. Do not leave them with a neighbor or immediate relative; these are some of the first people your abuser will go to!

- Take out a post-office box or a box at your local shipping store for your mail.
- If you have a restraining order, keep it handy at all times! Make your children's school aware of the order, and make sure that local law enforcement knows about the order. Provide extra copies to day-care providers and schools, if necessary.
- As embarrassing as it may be, let your employer know about your situation and what your abuser looks like. Have your work calls screened.
- Be prepared to have an escort with you at all times, including to and from your car, and so on.
- Do not isolate yourself or move to a secluded area.
- Secure your bank accounts. Change passwords and PIN numbers.
- If and when your budget allows, get a new computer (or borrow one from a friend) and a new cell phone number. Your old computer could have spyware installed that you are unaware of.
- Stay off social networks. You never know who may be friends with your abuser.
- Have pepper spray on you at all times (if the law allows).
- Consult a professional before you execute your plan.
- Seek out resources in your area for domestic-violence victims. These may include nonprofits or associations that can provide free resources and legal counsel if you need.

Exercise for Strategic Planning

There are many tools available via the internet based upon the desired outcome but a simple strategic plan involves these basic steps;

1. Where am I now? (Self-audit, analysis, research)
2. Where do I want to be? (Vision, goals, targets)
3. The Strategic Plan is the gap in between to bridge the gap. The gap can be one, three, or five years or can be broken down into smaller chunks of time like one month, three months, and six months depending upon the desired outcome.
4. Plan should be regularly examined and refined.

A Woman carries her shoes, but it's the shoe that carries the Woman.

—CHRISTIAN LOUBOUTIN

CHAPTER 10

Piecing Your Bag Together: Choosing Resilient Materials

How DO YOU SOLVE LIFE's problems? Do you think to yourself, "Am I going to ever get out of this problem?" or "Why do I have this problem in the first place?" Do say to yourself, "How am I going to solve this or fix this problem?"

My grandmother, Henrietta, was my primary caretaker from the time I was eight until I was sixteen. She always had this way of looking at things differently. She would encounter a problem, and instead of throwing a fit and crying about it, she would calmly look at the situation and say, "Hmm…let me think, how are we going to solve this problem?" She never said, "Are we going to solve this problem or why do we have this problem?" Her response always focused on the how. This was an empowering perspective for me. Sometimes she would come up with several different "how to" scenarios and then figure out which one was the easiest and most logical. She would invent some sort of gadget or create new solutions to problems in order to deal with whatever speed bump was in her way at the time. If she was short on cash, she would figure out a way to spend less or save from somewhere else. No matter what, she always found a way. This was my first introduction to problem solving.

For example, in our family she had a signature "fix" for saving money on wrapping paper. She would save the Sunday comics section and use it to wrap our presents. Now, granted, we all had black fingers after we were done opening our gifts, but it became an endearing memory and part of who she was.

My grandmother had a way of recycling everything. I thought it was a stroke of genius really, to take everything we used and recycle it in some way. From plastic bread bags to empty coffee cans, everything had a dual purpose. It was amazing how creative she could be! Plastic bread bags were used for storage, and empty coffee cans were transformed with twine into containers to pick blueberries or strawberries from the bushes on the farm. My grandmother had a way of magically transforming the most mundane item into something clever. She was "green" even before being green was cool! She also took her cod-liver oil every morning. When I was growing up, she always said, "It helps my joints." Now, this was long before Omega-3 compounds and chia seeds became popular.

Yep, my grandmother was a visionary and a pioneer. She used her instincts and intuition to solve problems. I would call her a trendsetter. I am sure she would never have thought of herself as a trendsetter, but looking back on everything she did and taught me, I can say with certainty that she was a woman before her time. From her beliefs about alternative medicine to her way of always fixing things, my grandmother thought outside the box and taught me to do the same.

Henrietta also had rebellious side. She went to nursing school in Hartford and commuted on the train during a time when a woman having a career outside the home was unheard of. She got married at twenty-nine to a man who was divorced, which was also unheard of at the time.

Even though my grandmother was a nurse at Saint Frances Hospital in Hartford for over twenty-five years, she swore by her chiropractor. One day when I was thirteen, I got off the bus and walked to her kitchen for milk and cookies as usual. Only on this particular day, she wasn't there to greet me.

"Get in the car!" my grandfather ordered. "We are taking your grandmother to the chiropractor. She threw her back out."

When my grandfather spoke, I listened and didn't ask questions. I made a beeline for the car. As they emerged from the house, I saw my grandfather carrying my grandmother on his back, piggyback style. *What in the hell?* As he slowly and carefully lowered my grandmother into the car, I noticed that she was crying. I fell silent. I had never—not ever—seen her cry before.

We rode in silence to the chiropractor's office, which was about a thirty-minute drive away. With the exception of my grandmother's whimpering, you could hear a pin drop. *Why aren't we going to the hospital?* I thought.

Out loud, I said, "Grandma, maybe we should take you to the hospital."

The rage in my grandmother's eyes at that moment is a look I will never forget. "What the hell are they going to do for me there besides give me a bunch of pills?"

Now I felt like complete idiot. I shrank back into the seat and kept my mouth shut for the rest of the ride.

What happened at the chiropractor's office was astounding. Since she was unable to walk in, my grandfather once again piggybacked her. Another thirty minutes went by, and then she walked out laughing and smiling. *What the heck just happened in there?* I wondered. I was blown away by the thought that by using only your hands, you could help someone in pain walk again. I was dumbfounded.

I forgot about this memory until my grandmother passed away. After she died, I felt like a rug was pulled out from under me. I had no direction and was at a dead-end job. I took time to do some soul-searching, and that is when I decided to become a chiropractor. I thought it was truly amazing to help people with just my two hands.

I never really thought of myself as having a rebellious side or being a rebel until I looked back on my life and realized why my grandmother would say that I was full of "piss and vinegar." When I heard that as a little girl, I thought, *Gross. What does that mean? I wonder if that is anything like being a pill.* I liked to think of myself as a strong-minded child with an avant-garde attitude; it just sounded more chic and sophisticated.

Looking back, I definitely had the "piss and vinegar" gene. My rebellious side started showing up when I was almost four years old. My younger brother was not born yet, so I was all on my own. I wanted to be an only child so bad. When my mom announced that she was going to have another baby, I thought that as the firstborn, I was entitled to name the baby. My mom didn't know it was a boy, but I had a feeling it would be, and I wanted to call him a good rebellious name. Tex seemed like the perfect fit. I thought that, if I had to have a brother, any brother of mine should be called Tex. My parents weren't buying it. So along came Peter.

Before Peter was born the following June, I was still all on my own for Christmas 1974. My parents always had a live tree that we would go chop down at a tree farm. Once the tree was ornately decorated with glass balls and tinsel—yes, tinsel…it was the 1970s…work with me—I was warned, "Amy, do not touch the tree."

Now my little brain could not figure out what purpose my not touching the tree would serve. Did my parents fear that it would fall down on me, or did they fear that I would break an ornament on it? I am still not sure. Every time I got near that beautiful, sparkly Christmas tree (I was drawn to sparkly things early on), my mother would shout from another room, "Amy, I can see you near that tree! Don't touch it!" How is it that all mothers develop eyes in the back of their heads?

Unfortunately for my parents, anytime I heard the words "don't" or "can't," my rebellious fire was fueled to figure out a way "how to." Don't forget, my grandmother taught me that the words "don't" and "can't" don't really exist. Don't forget, she taught me "how to". So my mom's words "Don't touch the tree" translated into "how to find a way to touch that sparkly tree without getting caught or breaking anything?" I decided that I would prove my mother wrong by touching the tree and not breaking anything. However, there was still a little voice inside me that told me not to disobey my mother.

Well, it was only a matter of time before the human spirit overtook me. I sat in my little chair for what seemed like hours staring at that tree and waiting for just the right moment—when my mother wasn't looking with the eyes behind her head—to touch that shiny Christmas tree. Sometimes she would even bring out the big guns and tell me, "Santa Claus is watching you, and if you touch that tree, you will be on the naughty list!"

Oh, the dreaded naughty list: no one wants to be on that around Christmastime. But my primal urge to do something I couldn't got the best of me. With just the very tip of my right index finger, I slowly reached out and with the gentlest touch, my finger met the tip of one of the lower branches. I did not know it, but my mother captured a photo of this moment.

My rebellious side manifested itself throughout my life. Whenever someone told me I couldn't do something, my mind shifted into one of two questions: "How can I make this happen?" or "How can I make it work?" I thought everyone's mind worked this way; I didn't even know that it was considered rebellious, resilient, or creative. Sure, I know that it was rebellious of me to touch the tree when I was told not to. But I did not want to be labeled a "rebel" by my family. When I thought of rebels, I thought of people acting on behalf of a personal cause or vendetta who may or may not be out to do harm to other people. To me, rebels acted inappropriately or illegally for a cause, and I did not want to be considered as such.

What I realize now is that this "rebellious" side of me can also be called my resilient side. When I think of resilience, I think of acting on my own behalf for my own good. Sure, I had my moments of true rebellion when I acted out like a brat or truly tested my boundaries, but I never got into any trouble. I was a considered a good, high-achieving kid who got good grades.

Resilience to me is that intangible "piss and vinegar" my grandmother made reference to. Resilience gives us the strength to keep going beyond ourselves. Resilience is the "how to make it work" and not the "will it work" mentality. It is what makes us do things and overcome odds we never thought possible. Now, I am no psychologist, but I would say that of all of the intangible assets I have, resilience is my most valuable. Before identifying my resilient spirit, if someone had asked me to describe myself in one word, I would have said that the word would have been "determined"— that I have determination. I now see that resilience is a more fitting adjective to describe me. Yes, determination is important, but the bounce-back, resiliency factor is equally important. Remember the trampoline analogy?

What can you do for yourself to change your mindset when you start thinking, *"What am I going to do?"* Instead of, *"How am I going to do it?"* How will your bag evolve if you begin to think this way and reprogram your thoughts when you catch yourself thinking from a pity standpoint? How will your bag begin to be pieced together differently, with more strength if you come from this perspective?

AFFIRMATION: I am selecting resilient materials for my life that support my new self and my new bag. I will figure out a way to make changes and progress toward my goals. I will surround myself with people who will support and encourage my how to mindset.

Exercise

Think about the following and write down the answers.

* What resilient materials do you have in your spiritual arsenal?
* Think of a time in your life when you felt most resilient. Write it down in detail. Write down what you were doing and wearing, and, more importantly, describe how you were feeling. Then when you feel vulnerable, pull it out and read it. Tap in to your resilient feelings. Use this exercise to visualize your strength to get you through your current situation.

Success is neither nature nor nurture.
Everyone can choose to change, grow, and succeed.

—*DARREN HARDY*

If you really want something, you'll find a way;
if you don't, you'll find an excuse.

—*JIM ROHN*

Nothing compares to the simple pleasures of riding a bike.

—*JOHN F. KENNEDY*

CHAPTER 11

One Stitch at a Time

HAVE YOU EVER NOTICED THAT sometimes the best things in life require patience and time? Do you ever just wish you had a magic wand so it could be done already? Creating a new bag from scratch requires time and patience, just like everything else in life. If you think about it, you'll probably realize that you started learning about patience in during your childhood. Have you ever had to stand in line for ice cream or to go on a ride? As a kid, it feels like forever and requires learning patience and persistence.

When I first learned how to ride a bike, my scarred elbows and knees were proof that I fell off more than I was on. I remember my first bicycle well. It had a purple metallic body with a white banana seat, and I called it Purple Streak. The chrome U-shaped handlebars were equipped with shredded plastic streamers adorning the white handles, and of course, what bike would be complete without a set of training wheels? My bike had those higher handlebars like the ones you see on what I would call a "hog" motorcycle. I felt so cool!

I remember getting on that bike for the first time and rocking it back and forth on the training wheels. Little did I know my father had put them on the highest setting. I guess he wanted me to learn fast. I had no idea that training wheels were actually supposed to touch the ground at first. I remember being six or seven years old and thinking it was unusual, but my dad knew best, so I didn't question it.

The first time I got the bike, I felt unsteady—you know that unsteady feeling you get when you try anything for the first time—and could not even pedal. I felt nervous, anxious, and excited all at the same time. My feet touched the pedals and I pushed with all my strength, but I could not get the wheels all the way around before I fell off and scraped my knee. Now, when I learned to ride a bike, I was not required to wear a helmet. (Hey, it was the 1970s.) Falling off didn't stop me, I got back up immediately. The next time I tried to pedal, I was able to do two and a half revolutions with the pedals before I fell off. Wow! I was getting it! I was riding a bike!

I again got back up, and now I was cooking. I closed my eyes and imagined myself pedaling Purple Streak all the way around the loop of the cul-de-sac. I opened my eyes, and, with this vision still in my head, I got going as fast I could pedal, imagining myself pedaling so fast that I was floating with my head held high, wind blowing through my hair, feeling as free as a graceful leaf in autumn being carried on the wind that was until I hit a large pothole. In that moment, all I can remember was the crashing sound that Purple Streak made as it—and I—hit the pavement.

What I forgot to learn was how to brake and how to steer properly. I was so excited to learn to ride Purple Streak, with the fancy hog handlebars, white banana seat, and training wheels, that I forgot one very important thing: learning how to steer and stop.

"I am never riding this bike again!" I screamed, stomping with closed fists and blood oozing from my top lip. I could feel my lip begin to swell and get warm. "This bike is terrible," I cried, trying to muster every word out of my now lisp-filled vocabulary. "I got hurt, and now I never want to ride that thing again!"

I remember my dad speaking softly, "Amy, it's not the bike's fault. Give it some time. All you need is some practice, and you will be riding that bike in no time."

Inside I was thinking, *Yeah, right; sure, Dad. As I said, I am never getting on that thing again. I don't care what you say.*

Well, once the swelling went down, and my ego recovered, I got back on Purple Streak slowly and cautiously this time, and with my dad's help.

He ran alongside me and held his hand out to catch me in case I fell. As he ran beside me, he spoke encouraging words, "You've got this; you can do it—I am right here."

If I pedaled at the right pace, my dad's hand even gently caressed my back as I moved along, and before you knew it, I was off, and my dad was just an image in the distance. I lapped around our neighborhood once. I could feel my vision of success begin to come to life. A warm feeling of confidence began to emerge.

When I got back to the driveway where my dad was waiting for me, he said, "How about we take those training wheels off now?"

"Do you think I am ready? I only went around once."

Proudly and confidently, my dad replied, "I know you are ready!"

Sometimes we all need a little assistance in life. Maybe it is a gentle nudge or a pat on the back. Maybe it's someone to run beside us when we aren't sure of ourselves or are facing something scary, like cancer. The truth is that when we learn about riding a bike, we are not just learning about riding a bike. We are also developing resilience, persistence, and patience; we're learning about getting back up time and again and brushing ourselves off when we scrape our knees or knock our teeth out. These are all valuable materials when you are reconstructing your handbag. Life is about getting back on the bike when you don't want to. Life is about having someone run beside you when you feel afraid. Learning to ride a bike teaches you confidence in yourself, and, once you learn, you never forget and can always get back on.

Riding a bike is a metaphor for living a life; by riding we learn to visualize success. Sometimes you have to keep on pedaling. Sometimes the wind will be at your face, and sometimes it will be at your back. The point is to keep pedaling. You will have to go up hills and down hills, steer clear of potholes and rocks, and even hit a speed bump or two. Keep pedaling. Sometimes you will go through forests and sometimes open road. Just keep pedaling. Sometimes you fall off and skin your knees. It's OK; we all do. Get up, brush yourself off, keep pedaling, and if you need to, wear a helmet.

Just like riding a bike, you might prick your finger on a needle, cut the wrong size fabric, or buy the wrong sized zipper when constructing your bag. The most important thing to remember is that it's ok to make some mistakes. It is how we learn and we get up and try again.

AFFIRMATION: I will get support on my journey if I need it, and I will keep "pedaling" no matter how many times I may want to give up.

I am creating my ideal bag patiently one stitch at a time.

Exercise

Think about these questions, and write down the answers.

* Who is in your corner or running beside you in life? Is it a mentor or spouse?
* Do you have someone in your life who you would call your "go to" person during times of stress or uncertainty?
* What potholes or speed bumps do you need to brace yourself for or steer clear of?
* Are your potholes and speed bumps people or circumstances?
* In what ways have you taken life one stitch at a time and practiced patience and persistence?

CHAPTER 12

Replacing the Contents One at a Time

WHEN IS THE LAST TIME you gave yourself a swift kick in the butt? "Pull yourself up by your bootstraps, girl!" This was another one of my grandmother's favorite expressions. It was her no-nonsense way of telling me to wipe my tears and pull myself together. You may have also heard the expressions, "Grow a backbone," "Get up, and dust yourself off," or even the dreaded, "Get thicker skin!" All of these tough-love approaches, as I call them, are the verbal equivalent of throwing a bucket of ice water over your head. They are calls to action.

The problem I had when I heard the bootstrap expression was that I didn't know how to grow a backbone, get thicker skin, or pull myself up. There were times in my life when I felt like I had been repeatedly kicked in the gut in a figurative sense and just wanted to stay down for fear of getting up and being kicked again. What I really needed during these times was a handbook or a guide to help me get back up. We all have the power to choose to get back up and keep on going. We also have personal choice to stay down for as long as we want. The only difference between those who get back up and try again and those who don't is resilience. It is what separates the men from the boys. This book is designed to help you find ways to not only be more resilient, but more importantly, to be the *most* resilient version of yourself you can be.

One of the most important aspects to getting your life back on track is the transformational work that involves the space between your ears. There are times in life when we all lack motivation, are missing inspiration, are having bad days, or are just plain depressed. Any such time calls for a swift kick in the butt! Sometimes the butt kick has to be a major conscious effort. At times, it needs to come from a close friend rather than yourself. That is OK! Sometimes you actually have to tell yourself to get out of bed or to go for that walk. The most important thing is just to get out of your own way.

Start somewhere! Sometimes your start can be as small as taking a five-minute walk. If you add to your efforts every day, before you know it, you will be up to a half hour! The first step is the hardest and the biggest! Sometimes all you can do is start with baby steps, but baby steps over time add up to a marathon! In the beginning, these small steps may feel like a chore, but over time they will become a joyful accomplishment when you see the results of your transformational work.

I learned this strategy intuitively and early on, with diet and exercise. Just recently, the concept became reinforced when I read Darren Hardy's book, *The Compound Effect*, in which he talks about how to make small, positive, incremental changes every day. These small steps will compound over time and result in major changes, whether in the area of financial freedom, fitness, diet, or something else.

Think about where you would be if you stopped watching a half hour of television per day and instead spent that half hour doing something that either brings you joy or has some other positive effect, like spending an extra thirty minutes with your kids, exercising, or reading inspirational books. By the end of one year, you will be much happier or more physically fit or better informed. What will the extra half hour of TV do for you? Absolutely nothing.

The opposite also holds true. Recall the scenario of gaining "only" one pound per year for ten years and then "discovering" the need to lose ten pounds. Again, imagine gaining one pound every year. Every day of that year, you would not notice you were gaining weight, and by the end of the year you would think, "Hey, not bad, I only gained a pound this year." But if that happened every year for ten years, then you would have gained ten pounds, would wonder why your pants no longer fit, and would think about trying to lose the weight. When you begin the process of trying to lose ten pounds, it may be much more difficult because you are ten years older and most likely have a slower metabolism, potentially poor eating habits, and a more sedentary lifestyle. Losing weight can then become a painstaking process that requires restriction, major modification, or life-style change, which most people find difficult, not to mention the potential emotional side effect of feeling restricted. Imagine if this example was applied with two or three pounds per year.

I used the baby-step technique to get through chiropractic school and life as a single mom (and even earlier, when I had to overcome my post-partum depression). During the roller-coaster ride of two and a half years after leaving Will in 2002, I felt that it would have been easy for me to lose focus on the big picture and just drop out of school altogether. I knew that most, if not all, of my friends and family would not have blamed me if I did. My commute to school was an hour and fifteen minutes one way, class began at 8:00 a.m. and lasted until 5:00 p.m. or 5:30 p.m.; then, by the time I got home, all I could do was eat, spend a few minutes with my daughters before they went to bed, study, and do homework. The next morning, I would get up and do it all over again. Day-to-day life was really no walk in the park.

Perspective and persistence are the two things that got me through. I would look at my life in a series of time increments, and this technique helped me get through in manageable pieces. I also figured that the time would pass anyway, whether I was following my dream or not. If I dropped out, I would feel like a miserable failure and be no closer to my dreams of becoming a doctor. I also put the ages of my daughters into perspective; I wanted to be done with school by the time they would really remember me being gone so much. It was important to me to have my schooling completed by the time their memories were more developed, so that I would be there for them.

Hour by hour, day by day, I persisted. Every day I got one step closer to completing my dream to become a doctor. Day after day, one piece at time, a more resilient section was placed back into my bag. My bag was getting stronger and I was adding quality contents.

AFFIRMATION: I am constantly keeping my focus on the big picture and taking steps everyday toward my goals.

Exercise

Think about these questions, and write down the answers.

* What mental or emotional building blocks can you begin to rein-force on a daily basis?
* How can you break down a task or situation into chewable bites of time?
* When were there times in your life when you persevered with persistence?
* Sign up for daily inspiration. The Internet is full of websites for this.
* Keep your eye on the big picture and not just on a day-to-day perspective.

Body confidence is when you honor your body for being the home to an incredible soul.

—JESSICA ORTNER

CHAPTER 13

Care Instructions

ARE YOU READY TO CARE for you bag and protect your investment? So, you have designed your new bag, chosen resilient materials, assembled it one stitch at time, and replaced the contents, now it is time to take proper care of it! At this point, you have invested time, energy, effort, and maybe money into your masterpiece which means caring for it and maintaining it is critical to protect your investment. Part of this process requires honoring your body, mind, and spirit as you move forward on your journey. Honoring your body means taking care of it from the inside out along with your mind and spirit. Honoring your body also means taking time for self-care in all of the various forms that takes, including exercise, diet, and lifestyle habits.

Honoring my body in the form exercise was a struggle for me at times. I was always an active kid, and I played three sports in high school. But I have to admit, I never really loved to exercise. In my adult life, I have gone through periods of time when I would work out in fits and starts, and struggle with motivation. As a genetically thin person, I would hear comments like, "You don't have to work out; you're so thin!" I have had exercise-induced asthma from childhood, so any cardiovascular activity would turn into a struggle for air until I got into my mid-thirties and learned how to manage the asthma with proper diet and proper cardio.

The word "exercise" itself would actually invoke a feeling of anxiety and dread. Even though I am thin and most people assume I work out, working out to me triggered memories of my days of conditioning practice with my high-school volleyball team. My coach would make me run until I vomited, hyperventilated, passed out, or suffered some various combinations of all of these. I used to think she was purposely torturing me to test my resilience. Either way, running or exercise to me equaled torture and a date with a brown paper bag.

So when I hit my mid-thirties, realized that I was not getting any younger, and noticed that my arms had developed a jiggle that made me uncomfortable, I decided that it was time to start exercising again. I went with the take-it-slow approach: for the first day, exercise for ten minutes, and then build on that. I honestly hated every minute, but by the end of ten minutes, I thought, *OK, not so bad, and I feel kinda good.*

Eventually, I worked up to thirty to forty minutes of intermittent running followed by short walking intervals so I did not hyperventilate. I learned to use my inhaler before physical activity. Why no one told me that trick earlier in my life, I am not sure. Still, during that entire time period, my mind-set with regard to exercise was, *This sucks, and it's torturous and painful.*

Day after day, my mind-set was the same. One day, I would skip my exercise routine, and then one day would turn into two. Two days would turn into a week, and, before I knew it, a whole year had gone by and I gradually stopped altogether.

Then I hit thirty-nine, and, with the big four-o looming, I decided that this time I was going to get into the best shape of my life. With a newly determined mind-set, I started working out and cleaning up my diet with unrelenting passion. My drive to be in the best shape of my life outweighed that nagging voice in my head that kept saying, *This is painful torture.* Well, at least it did for about eight months.

But for those eight months, I diligently read through every fitness blog and all the articles on Bodybuilding.com. I ate more egg whites in a single day than I ever had in one week. No doubt some readers will say that the thought of eating egg whites twice a day would be torture enough, but to me it was all part of the bigger picture. I was going to be a fit, over-forty model, and I was going to compete in a fitness competition.

Why I thought I would do that was beyond me, but, at the time, it seemed feasible. Guess what? I fell off the wagon once again, because my mind-set about exercise hadn't made a necessary shift yet.

One day about six months ago, I went over to a friend's house for lunch to work on a project. As we were sitting at her computer, I looked up and noticed a horizontal piece of paper with a table on it and boxes for the days of the week. At the top of the paper were the words: **Honor Your Body**. For each day, she had written her goals and a schedule of which physical activities she wanted to do on what days. It was all laid out. Seeing those words on her "exercise log" struck at the heart of a personal struggle for me. I didn't say anything to her at the time because we were in a creative flow with our project, and so I filed my thoughts away for later.

After I had gotten home, eaten dinner, and was getting ready for bed, I remembered her piece of paper. The words "Honor Your Body" kept resonating in my head. I thought, *Maybe if I change my perspective about exercising and eating well from a place of pain and torture to this place of choosing to honor my body, then I will be more inspired to take consistent action and make consistent choices toward honoring the body that God gave me.*

It seemed like a light bulb was shining in my brain! I had spent my entire life fighting the inner demons that surrounded diet and exercise and the voices of shame and guilt that emerged whenever I would make unhealthy choices about my body and what I put into it. When during postpartum depression I had used food to comfort myself from the pain, I had struggled. On one shoulder an angel whispered, "You should exercise because it is good for you," while on the other shoulder, a demon said, "Exercise is torture and pain. Your lungs will hurt, and exercise is hard." Even though I was thin on the outside, my inner struggle was real, but no one knew it.

Changing my perspective toward making diet and exercise choices in the interest of honoring my body felt much more freeing to me and was a quantum leap in my mindset around this. The shame and guilt around this topic were gone for the first time, and I felt free from the stranglehold my mind-set had imposed on me. I felt free from the deep internal mental conditioning I had endured in high school. Choosing to honor my body felt empowering. It took me a few days of internalizing and chewing on this idea to comprehend fully what the words "Honor Your Body" meant to me.

Honoring your body will mean something different to each person. It can mean getting enough sleep or slowing down when life is taking you at a hundred-miles-an-hour pace. It can mean having that single cookie without guilt or not having the cookie without feeling deprived. Either way, the freedom to choose to honor your body is deeply empowering. Choosing to have a rest day from physical activity is also honoring your body. Honoring your body means taking care of it with reverence for the vessel it is because it is housing a magnificent gift, your soul.

Honoring your body directly connects to honoring your soul and spirit by taking care of it, tending to it, and paying attention to what it needs every day. The concept of honoring our bodies and spirits prompts me to think about the sexual and physical abuse that sometimes accompanies domestic-violence situations; choosing to honor yourself and your body means making difficult choices that involve confronting or leaving an abusive situation. Honoring our bodies for some can mean choosing to be free from the grip of addiction. These choices are not at all easy. You will have to be committed and ready for change to take place. What may make the changes easier is to think about changing your perspective from a mind-set of feeling pain and torture to a mind-set of making an empowering choice to honor yourself. Treating your body, mind, and spirit with dignity can be freeing, as it was for me.

It is amazing to me how much impact a simple act of changing one's perspective can have on how one views his or her life. Changing perspective has been one of the most valuable tools I have learned during my resilience process. Sometimes we can't do this for ourselves. We need the help of a friend or a divine inspiration. It's OK. You don't have to figure it out alone. As the saying goes, "When the student is ready, the teacher appears." Be on the lookout for teachers. Be in the moment. Honor your body.

Nurture yourself whenever possible. Honoring your body, mind, and spirit is the beginning of building a resilient inner framework. Honoring your newly designed masterpiece (a.k.a. your new handbag) will help support you and your new future. Whenever you put something in your mouth or have a negative thought, ask yourself, "Does this honor me, my spirit, and my body?" If the answer is no, then you probably should think twice about whatever it is. Your body, mind, and spirit are a temple.

Caring for and beautifying your appearance also honors your body, mind, and soul as well as the divine within you. In doing so, you are sending this message to the universe: "Thank you for giving me this healthy body and mind. I will honor them and I take care of them. I will dress in clothes that make me feel like the masterpiece I am. I will feed my brain with positive thoughts and feed my body with healthy food that nourishes every cell."

Caring for yourself also means aligning your body, mind, and spirit. Aligning these three facets of yourself is important for physical, spiritual, and emotional congruency. Incongruities manifest themselves as disease, dysfunction, and physical pain. Past emotional traumas and present stress manifest themselves as dysfunction in the body and can lead to digestive problems, pain, muscle spasms, and overall fatigue, just to name a few examples. Dealing with past emotional traumas and stressors is an important part of healing and alignment of the spiritual, emotional, and physical body. I have found this to be true in my private practice, and I will talk more about this later on.

ALIGNING THE PHYSICAL BODY

Alignment of the physical body actually begins with what you put into it for fuel. Just as you would put the highest grade of gasoline into a high-performance race car, you should eat plenty of fruits, colorful vegetables, and lean protein—the basis for a healthy lifestyle—to keep your body running in tip-top shape. After all, you want your engine running at its peak performance so that you can do your best work. Keeping your body healthy means you can heal quicker, bounce back quicker, have greater stamina, and enjoy a more powerful immune system to fight disease. Having a diet and lifestyle full of inflammatory substances lowers your body's ability to fight disease, adds to oxidative stress, and diminishes peak performance.

Think about this way. Your body is like a high-performance car such as a Porsche or Ferrari. You would not put low-quality gasoline or oil in car like that, now would you? Your body deserves to be treated the same way. Why? Because you are even more precious than the luxury vehicle. Remember that your body is the vehicle that houses your spirit and keeps it mobile. Honoring your body and what you put in it and on it are ways to honor the divine in you, so avoid all CRAP which is an acronym for the following:

*   **Carbohydrates:** To clarify, I'm talking about "simple" carbo-hydrates (carbs). Avoid all white bread, white rice, and anything made with white flour. Our bodies get plenty of carbs from fresh fruits and vegetables. By consuming those, we will never be carb deficient.
*   **Refined sugar:** Simple, refined sugar is an inflammatory culprit and also gets stored as fat if it is not used right away. It has also been called a "feeder" to many cancers.
*   **Artificial sweeteners:** These substances have been shown to be toxic to the nervous system.
*   **Processed foods:** Processed foods are also inflammatory and can lead to cardiovascular disease and other health issues.

Physical alignment of the body also involves unsticking your inner energy and divine purpose. Physical alignment in this sense includes gentle chiropractic care, massage, and acupuncture. Alignment can also come in the form of yoga, Pilates, Reiki, and other healing forms of movement. As a chiropractor, I am an advocate of manually aligning the spine using a variety of gentle, conservative techniques. I think this is the most efficient and effective way to achieve dramatic results quickly.

Your spine is the physical and spiritual representation of your foundation. It is like the foundation of your house. What happens to your house if the foundation is not level? Over time, walls crack and settle. Sometimes doors won't even close. Floors and ceilings become sloped. If the foundation of the house is not level to begin with, nothing above that will be level either. The same holds true for your body; if your spine and pelvis are not level, your biomechanics will not function properly. You will experience muscle strain, and, over time, your joints will become arthritic because of the uneven stress, strain, wear, and tear.

Physical alignment signifies that your spine is healthy and functioning optimally for you. In Chinese medicine, there is a life force or "chi" that flows through the meridians of your body. The Chinese believe that the chi is carried through your blood stream. In energy-work practices, the chakras (energy centers) are also believed to carry a flow of energy and need to be in alignment. When the spine and body are healthy and in alignment, this energy or life force also is free flowing and dynamic.

Think of it this way: if you had a bottle half full of water, held it horizontally, and then rocked it between your left and right hand, the water would flow freely back and forth, circulating the water. Now imagine that same bottle of water was bent in the middle, representing a misalignment. The water would not flow smoothly back and forth through the bottle, would it? It would get stuck on either end. The same is true of the fluid in your spine and the energy in your body. Kinks or misalignments can be physical, emotional (stress-based), or mental blocks. Blocks or stagnation keep energy, ideas, and creativity stuck, which leads to feeling "unsettled," anxious, unfulfilled, achy, and so on.

HONORING YOUR MIND AND SPIRIT

When I began thinking about the content for this part of the book, I found that talking and writing about the mind, body, and spirit connection feels very foreign and messy to me. I feel vulnerable talking about it. Putting my emotions in compartments has served me well over the years. I like having everything in order, neat, and perfectly packaged. I like things that make logical sense. I am much more of an analytical, scientifically oriented person and less of an esoteric, spiritual type of person. Throughout my life, I have found it easier to shove my feelings under the rug because they were too messy and painful to talk about. The mind and spirit stuff is ethereal and outside the boxes of compartmentalization I am comfortable with.

So talking about meditation and spiritual stuff is uncharted territory for me. Since I am neither an expert on these subjects nor a therapist, I will not address the philosophical mind and spirit connection, I will stick to how the connection applies to how you look, feel, and view yourself, and leave more complicated aspects of the subject to the professionals. I do, however, want to touch on these two areas of meditation and spirituality. Many of the references I will use and tips I will give can be used for both, so it will be easier to talk about the two together.

I have done my fair share of soul-searching over the years. Have you ever experienced such loss or transition that you started asking yourself, "Is there more to my life? What am I here for?" This is what I would call "soul-searching." It begins with a divine voice inside you calling you to do more and to be more, to stretch yourself, for example. Crazy as it may sound, I have had conversations with this voice many times, even while writing this book. It is important to tap into that voice—it's your soul talking. Are you listening? Have you stopped long enough in your busy life to hear it? If not, I would suggest that you do. We are all here on this planet for a greater purpose. What is yours? How can you find your purpose in life? The fact is that you need to ask yourself that question and use your intuition.

Whenever I have a difficult decision to face, or I am at a fork in the road and don't know what direction to take, I pray and meditate and have a conversation with God and my inner child, asking what I should do next. Connecting to that inner child has always guided me in an unbiased direction. Think about it. Little children are innocent and bias-free.

They are carefree and open with their ideas and opinions before someone eventually comes along and tell them that they "can't" or they are not "good enough," or "smart enough," and so on. As children we are more connected to our divine nature and what God has intended for us than we are as adults because of the adult ego and responsibilities. Ask your inner child what to do, and you will receive an honest, unbiased opinion. That inner child represents your soul. What is it saying to you?

Someone told me once that she had no desires or dreams for her life. I did not believe her. We all have desires and dreams. We have to ask our inner child and our divine Creator for answers. Sometimes the answers don't come easily. Sometimes we aren't meant to have all the answers right away. God wants us to be patient for his timing and have faith. Like children, we need to ask more questions. Be curious! Be innocent! Have faith! Pretend you have not been hurt yet. Pretend you are free with nothing to lose. You may need to reach out to a really great counselor, mentor, or friend for advice and direction once your soul answers.

Stay in touch through prayer and meditation with that inner calling and notice how you feel. To ignore it or to be out of alignment with it means you will experience feelings of disconnection and discontent. As you begin to see more and more clearly what your life's purpose is, you will realize that all of life's twists and turns were put in your path for a reason. You may not have known it at the time, but each and every circumstance has brought you to precisely where you are today. Listening to that inner childlike voice allows for growth and expansion and infinite possibilities. Being in touch with those infinite possibilities and your dreams further nurtures the divine in you.

What can you do to honor your body and spirit? A great way to honor your spirit is to tap into what you already love to do or seek out whom you love to work with. One of the ways I tap into my soul is with "art." Now, I am not an artist, but I do a pretty mean doodle. Doodling is therapeutic and meditative for me. Coloring can also be therapeutic and there are many adult coloring books out there. For some of you, it may be cooking or reading. Maybe you love to get massages or listen to spa music. Whatever activity nurtures your spirit, by all means do it as long as it is not harmful to anyone else.

AFFIRMATION: I am taking steps every day to honor my body, mind, and spirit by making healthy choices that I feel good about.

I am in daily conversation with my inner child, the Divine, and my intuition to check my steps and path.

Exercise

Think about these questions, and write down the answers.
Consider the following questions to determine the best ways to honor your body (yes, I said it without hyperventilating):

* What do you do for yourself to honor your body every day?

* What behaviors or attitudes do you have about making healthy choices that may be holding you back?

* What patterns are ingrained in you that you can begin to look at and change your perspective on?

* What support do you need to start honoring your body?

* Visualize what honoring your body means to you. What actions are you taking?

Consider the following questions to determine the best ways to honor your mind and spirit:

* If you are held back because you lack knowledge or feel overwhelmed, who can you reach out to for teaching or coaching?

* What resources do you have available?

* What practices and new patterns can you do for five to ten minutes per day to honor your mind and spirit?

* What desires or dreams do you have?

* What message is your soul speaking to you?

* What activities do you do to honor your soul (e.g., meditation, art, music, and so on)?

A Few Tips about Eating Healthier

* **Maximize cooking time:** Always cook extra for leftovers, for great additions to salads and omelets. Use your evening meal as part of your lunch for the next day. For example, grilled chicken for dinner can be used as your protein for your salad at lunch.

* **Use healthy fats:** Cook with olive oil or a healthy alternative. Olive oil provides monounsaturated fats (the good fat), but be aware of serving sizes: one tablespoon contains as many as 120 calories.

* **Experiment with new herbs and condiments:** Herbs are packed with flavor without calories; they can have powerful effects on our bodies and contain healing benefits. For example, ginger and parsley are excellent for digestion. Condiments like hummus, spices, vinegars, vegetarian spreads, and mustard can all provide flavors to keep your palette happy.

* **Select fruits and vegetables in season:** Fresh fruit and vegetables in season will taste better and usually be more affordable. Keeping up with the demand for fresh produce can be difficult in the winter months, so keep a liberal supply of frozen veggies on hand. Stock up when you see weekly sales.

* **Go nuts:** Nuts and seeds are an excellent source of healthy fat and fiber, not to mention quick and easy snacks. These should be raw and unsalted. Keep servings in snack bags or measure out to keep portions in check.

* **Select protein wisely:** Knowing the quality of the meat you are eating is important. Ideally, you should look for lean meats that are organic and/or free range (including organic free-range eggs).

* **Consider Omega-3s:** Incorporating fish into the diet is the best way to increase your good fats. Omega-3s facilitate an anti-inflammatory environment in the body, assist in mood stability, increase brain function, benefit cardiovascular health, and increase sensitivity to insulin in the body. Other vegetarian sources to look for

are chia, hemp, and flaxseed. They are an excellent supplement that maximizes your benefit for your dollar.

* **Cook simply:** Roast, broil, grill (careful not to burn), poach, steam, use broth to sauté, and moisten without oil.
* **Strategize:** Success comes a lot easier when you have some food ready to go in the fridge for fast and easy meal preparation.
* **Cook with nonstick pans, and use wooden utensils:** This reduces the amount of oil needed for cooking.
* **Combat hunger:** Use low carb vegetables for snacking and with any meal. They will provide fullness, fiber, and antioxidants without a lot of extra calories.
* **Check ingredients of breads and wraps:** Look for breads and wraps with high amounts of fiber. Remember: the more fiber and protein you see, the better! Read your labels. Low-carb bread should be about forty to forty-five calories per slice and wraps about ninety calories per serving.

A FEW MORE TIPS FOR SUCCESSFUL LIFESTYLE CHOICES;

* **Eating awareness:** Often we eat for many reasons other than hunger, such as stress, emotions, or habit. Do certain events or stress cause you to want to eat? Pay attention to how you feel when you eat or when you get cravings and identify what feelings you are having and why. This process will help you adjust your thinking, pause, and maybe even allow enough time to pass so that you don't reach for the chips when you feel stressed.
* **Keep hydrated:** Water stimulates metabolism and detoxifies the body. Often people mistake being hungry for being thirsty.
* **Slow it down:** It takes twenty minutes for your stomach to tell your brain that you are full. Take your time eating, and chew your food.

- **It's all about the portions:** Make sure you are eating the right size portion, and train your eyes to discern how much you should be eating. Foods such as nuts can be high in calories, so portion them into small portable bags to avoid eating too much.

- **Journal, journal, journal!** Journaling your food is critical to your success and the hardest part of staying on track in the beginning of a healthier lifestyle change but it will keep you accountable and show you what you're eating!

- **Stay active:** Do some sort of physical activity every day. If time is a factor, find fifteen to twenty minutes every day to go for a walk. It is easy to squeeze in a vigorous twenty-minute walk versus an hour at the gym. Consistency is key to weight loss and will also improve your mood. (Remember The Compound Effect I mentioned earlier?)

- **Eat every three hours:** Also, never skip breakfast because breakfast gets your metabolism revved up for the rest of the day.

- **Create balanced meals and snacks:** Be sure to have a little protein or fat in each meal, which will keep you satisfied and full.

- **Eat lots of vegetables:** Ideally, your dinner plate should always be half (or more) filled with veggies.

- **Eat foods that are in season:** They taste better, are more economical, and create harmony within the body.

- **Keep a *no*-fail environment:** The secret to success is to create an environment free from the foods that tend to tempt you. If you buy it, chances are one day you will eat it!

The show must go on.

—*Anonymous*

CHAPTER 14

Walking the Red Carpet

How WOULD YOU FEEL IF you could walk the red carpet on Hollywood's biggest night? Imagine for a minute how you would feel. Would your shoulders be back with your head held high being the picture of glamour and confidence? How would it feel to know that everything you worked so hard for was being recognized in a big way? Imagine emerging from the limousine with all of your biggest fans and supporters clapping and cheering for you.

Four years after my divorce was final, I was finally ready to get back into being social again. I had spent four years in a cocoon of self-deprecation, self-analysis, and introspection; I felt so ashamed and publicly humiliated that I did not want to show my face to the outside world. I felt ashamed for letting myself be treated in such a way. I felt ashamed that the public had seen such chaotic, embarrassing moments. I was safe in my inner sanctum, working on putting the pieces of me back together, my new bag, and my life. I became ultra-private. I decided just to hide and try not to stand out until I thought enough time had passed and I was ready to slowly make my way back out into being social again. Only this time, my bag was ready and I was fully equipped to step out as my new and improved self.

Even though I had a fledgling business that required me to market my skills and myself, I stayed in my private world. I would go to work, come home, make dinner, watch TV, and repeat, day after day. For a while, I was happy soaking in the peace and tranquility that came with the space to be by myself and spend time with my girls. On the other hand, that inner little girl who performed in front of her kindergarten class felt alone and isolated. I wondered if the real me would ever return. Staying quietly hidden and not drawing attention to myself is what kept me safe.

All people process life and events differently. Some people automatically call everyone they know to tell them what is going on and get opinion after opinion on what to do. I have friends who need to be social all of the time. They put themselves out there at every turn, and when faced with a difficult situation such as divorce or cancer, they instantly pick up the phone, call their friends, or hop on social media which unleash a team of support and help right away. At times I wonder whether they are so uncomfortable being by themselves that they need the validation of others, or they are just better at asking for help. I would like to understand their perspective with regard to dealing with life's struggles.

My reaction is the opposite. I turn inward—that is, I withdraw into the quiet depths of my own inner analyzer. My first question to myself is, *OK, What am I going to do now?* All of this accounts for a second reason that I spent three years in my quiet isolated cocoon of shame. Not only was I actually enjoying my peace and quiet, but I was also being introspective, trying to figure out what I wanted to do next in my life. I needed time to process and figure it out.

There were problems associated with choosing to stay hidden for a while. One problem was that my business required me to be a known entity to the public, so that I could bring in clients. In addition, being tall and attractive made it difficult to go unnoticed in public. It just didn't happen. Part of me really wanted to be invisible while the inner part of me yearned to be noticed. I love having an audience—not because I am self-absorbed but because I truly believe I have something to offer and share with the world.

I am a huge Harry Potter fan. My favorite magical aid was his cloak of invisibility. Boy, do I wish I had that! I suppose this is ironic coming from someone who loved being on stage as girl and being visible. I love the idea of having control over my own invisibility and being able to take it off around people I am comfortable with or at my choosing. If only life were like that. I would have spent three years with that cloak on and thought nothing of it, happily going about my routine day after day, going unnoticed. "Going unnoticed" meant that I wouldn't draw attention to myself and that I wouldn't have to hear, from my daughters, what their father or anyone else in town was saying about me behind my back. I also wouldn't have to defend myself for the way I lived my life or the shoes I wore. I guess I thought that if I were invisible, then those problems would just go away. I would be left with my real friends and family; they were the ones who truly cared, and they would check on me anyway.

My neighbor Kathy became my closest friend and confidant during this time. She was fifty-nine and divorced. She grew up in Connecticut and was a retired teacher. In her apartment, she had an entire wall of bookcases from the floor to the ceiling, filled with books. She was an avid reader and an accomplished sailor, having navigated much of the globe via sailboat. She was the first person who taught me about creating a vision board.

One day, over several glasses of wine, she told me a story about how she had mapped out on paper her five-year life plan when she was fifty-five down to every last detail. She cut out pictures from magazines of the house she wanted to live in England, the man she wanted to meet, and the sailboat she wanted. She had every detail of her life envisioned and mapped out. She had vacations to Bermuda, Thailand, France, and Mexico all on there. She listed people she wanted to meet, and even specified a pet, a black Labrador.

Now, let me refresh your memory. I grew up being influenced primarily by a woman who was, by her own accounts, a conservative Connecticut Yankee and devoted Christian. So vision boards sounded like a lot of mumbo jumbo to me. Vision boards were for dreamers, not doers. I was a doer, a high achiever. What did I need with a vision board? Nothing tangible could ever come from it, right? Or could it?

As we sat chatting that day and talking about her vision board, Kathy recounted to me how every detail of her vision board over the past five years had come true. I remember feeling stunned and amazed that this could be possible. She showed me pictures of trips she took to Bermuda and famous people she met. I was dumbfounded. I sat there at her antique, round oak table mesmerized by her words and the idea that there could actually be something to this vision board "thing." She explained how she pored over every detail of the man she would marry and the qualities he would have, that he would be an Oxford or Cambridge graduate and that he would love to sail and travel. She even wrote down that he would love a black Labrador.

Then she told me something I never thought she would say. She told me about how she met a man from England online and she was going over there to meet him. He had all of the qualities she described and had graduated from Cambridge! She had spent the past five years traveling back and forth to London to see him. I thought she was crazy. To be almost sixty years old and dating someone in a foreign country? "Are you nuts?" I asked her.

Her hearty laugh made me laugh, too. Maybe it was the wine, but we laughed until there were tears rolling down our cheeks. Then she composed herself and very seriously said to me, "Maybe I am crazy, but if you don't have a vision for your life, you'll have to take what you get, because the universe does not know what you want."

This was something I had never heard before. I had to really think about this, soak it in, and digest it. Kathy taught me so much that day about stepping out and living my dreams. She held my hand while I got back into socializing and trusting people. She helped me to see that life is good and people are good.

After I spent a few days really pondering what she said about the vision board, I decided to try it myself. But I thought I would start "small" with a list of qualities and characteristics titled, "The Man of My Dreams." I thought, *Hey, she has confidence that this thing will work, so why not put it to a real test? After all, I don't really believe in all this universe stuff.*

I wrote three lined notebook-paper pages of must-have qualities and qualifications for the "Man of My Dreams." Then I sat back and thought,

Ha, take that universe! Try to make that one come true! I had every single detail written down about how this man looked and what he valued. I wrote down what his career would be, how many kids he would have, that he was a non-smoker, and that he had sense of humor. I even wrote down what he would love most about me and what he would love most about my daughters. I wrote down that he would be able to help me in my business and would be loving and supportive of my dreams and goals. I wrote down that he would love me unconditionally and not judge my past. I wrote page after page of painstaking detail about my dream man. The <u>only</u> detail I left out was his hair color. I really thought I had set the bar too high for even God to make this one happen. My inner skeptic was getting ready for victory. I thought, *Never in a million years is this going to work.*

Two weeks later I met Matt, the man of my dreams. And guess what? Matt is bald.

As for Kathy, she is currently living happily in London, traveling the world, and married to the Cambridge man of her dreams (the same online friend she had told me about during our discussion). They are living in the same English cottage she cut out of the magazine with her black Labrador, George.

AFFIRMATION: I have a clear vision for my future down to every detail and am open to receiving abundance and happiness freely. I am holding this vision tightly in my mind and working towards it every day.

Exercise

Create your own vision board:

- Get a large, white poster board, some magazines, some markers, and anything else you may want to add to your board for inspiration. Block off two hours (uninterrupted) to create your vision board in a quiet space, free from distractions. You may even need to go to a friend's house if you can't focus in your own space. Before you begin, use this centering and connecting technique I learned: Take a deep breath to the count of five. Hold your breath to the count of five, and then blow out all the air again for five counts. You can also say a prayer if you wish.

- Imagine this board as your menu for your life. What do you want to put on it? Vacation spots? Cars? Do you want to be a best-selling author? Visualize every detail you can think of. What color car do you want, and when will you get it? What accomplishments do you want to achieve? Do you want to go back to school? If so, where will you go and what will you study? Think about where you want to live and what the house looks like. What kind of pet will you have? What will you look like? Will you have you lost weight? Who will be in your life? How do you feel as your future self? Write down these feelings, too! Do you feel more confident or empowered?

- You may also want to write down inspirational quotes on your board. Do you have a large circle of friends? What will your new handbag look like? What will your hairstyle be? What are you wearing as your future self? Use your imagination!

- This board is your opportunity to design your life however you may choose. Don't worry about thinking that your vision is too big. If you dream it, God put your dream there for a reason. Put it—all of it—down on paper.

- When you are done, put your name and the current date on the board.

If there ever comes a day when we can't be together,
keep me in your heart, I'll stay there forever.

—*Winnie the Pooh*

CHAPTER 15

Losing Your Valuables

NOVEMBER 21, 2012, WAS THE day a call came that I never expected. "Amy, Colin is gone." Those were the words that my brother Peter solemnly spoke.

"What do you mean he's gone? You mean missing? You're joking, right?"

"No, this isn't a joke. He passed away."

Colin was born November 30, 2007, one month premature via caesarean section in Tucson, Arizona. Peter and Kathy were as excited as all new parents are. They were beginning their life together and were moving into a new house in the midst of Colin's birth. So many happy and exciting changes were happening, and their future together as a family seemed bright—until two weeks later.

It was a warm December day in Tucson. Peter and Kathy were moving into a new condo to have more room for their new family. Peter was moving furniture from their old apartment into their new condo on the opposite side of Tucson. When he arrived home after his last back-and-forth trip of the day, he found Kathy's body on the floor of their apartment with two-week-old Colin in his car seat crying. Peter called 911, and when the paramedics arrived, they were able to revive Kathy. Kathy was rushed to the emergency room in Oro Valley and diagnosed with a massive heart attack. She was placed in a medically induced coma on life support and survived for only five days.

After Kathy passed away, Peter did the only thing that made sense: move back to Connecticut to get the support of his family to help him raise Colin. Right away, the family took turns traveling back and forth to Arizona to help Peter pack and tie up the loose ends so he could move back. My mom and I flew out to Arizona to fly back to Connecticut with Colin; Peter had decided to make the cross-country road trip to try to clear his head.

It's interesting how people assumed that my brother was a divorced, single dad whenever he went anywhere with Colin. It broke our hearts to know the truth. Peter, Colin, and my mom created a new life together. We all helped him heal after Kathy's death. Watching Colin grow up and take his first steps was a joy. As my only biological nephew, he was like the son I never had. He loved the girls, and the girls loved him. They were like his big sisters. They would share imaginative stories and "Scooby snacks" (a.k.a. fruit snacks). Colin talked with a little bit of lisp at first, and the girls would help him with pronunciation.

Colin loved three things more than anything: Tinkertoys, Iron Man, and his daddy. He was a bright little boy. From the age of six months, he loved puzzles and putting things together. He could do puzzles faster than the adults trying to help him. He had an amazing gift for spatial relationships.

Another thing he loved to do, as most kids do, was blow bubbles. There was a container of bubbles in just about every room and under the kitchen sink. He had special bubble-blowing guns along with the usual boring wands found in the containers. He and the girls would spend countless summer hours blowing bubbles and chasing them in the grass. Something about blowing bubbles makes you happy inside. Think about it: it's hard to be angry while you are blowing bubbles.

One of the last times I saw Colin alive was the last week of October 2012. I remember it vividly. He and I were playing on the floor with Tinkertoys, a K'Nex/Hasbro building system comprised of wooden wheel-shaped disks with holes drilled around their perimeters, and stick-like dowels that fit into the wooden disks. I was watching him intently putting the dowels into the holes of the wooden disk. When he was finished, it looked like a sun or the spokes of a bicycle.

"Colin, that is an awesome sun you made!"

He gave me this look as if to say, *Huh? What are you talking about?* Out loud, he said, "Auntie Amy, that's not a sun. It's an arc reactor! I am Tony Stark!"

Life from a four-and-a-half-year-old's perspective is much different from ours. In that moment with Colin, I was awestruck by the difference and the innocence of his imagination. In his head, he was the superhero, Iron Man, and his alter ego, Tony Stark. *Wow.* I thought to myself. *How wonderful it must be to live in his imagination instead of my own very literal interpretation of his Tinkertoys sculpture, which to me looked like the spoke of bicycle wheel or the rays of a sun.*

In the story of Iron Man, the arc reactor acted as Tony Stark's heart and thus kept him alive. After Colin's death, his Tinkertoys sculpture became a symbol of a resilience and strength in our family legacy. I spoke at Colin's funeral. I told the story of our playing with the Tinkertoys and said that the real Iron Man in all of this is my brother, Peter.

Handling major trauma, like the death of a child, takes time. I am convinced that the amount of time is different for everybody. Emotional wounds like this one change you forever. You look at things differently. Personally, I look at little boys I see in public differently. There are no rules, in months or even years. People who judge the length of time it takes you to process your own grief are not there to support you. All people handle grief in their own way and in their own time. It is easy to tell someone to get help right away or to "go see someone" during times like these. However, sometimes the pain needs time to be processed. It takes time to be ready to share your innermost painful feelings. Sometimes you wonder how much good talking about it will do.

The autopsy shed some light on Colin's untimely death. He had a rare spontaneous intestinal rupture of unknown cause while he was sleeping There were no signs or symptoms, no fever or diarrhea. He went to bed a normal four-and-a-half-year-old boy, but he did not wake up.

The autopsy only gave us the medical answers; it didn't provide us with the answers we really wanted. Why did someone so young have to die? What was the reason? Why did Peter have to lose Kathy and Colin? There were so many questions and no answers. The grief was overwhelming for all of us.

It took me almost two years to be able to talk about the ordeal. Even then, I had to take baby steps in talking about it. During the first year or so after this happened, I just felt lost and numb, like a hollow shell going through the motions of life, just as I had done so many other times in my life. But this time it was different; I sensed that something inside me had shifted.

Perhaps you have lost a child or other loved one and will need help with the grieving process when you are ready. I wanted so badly to blame God for taking Colin away from us, especially from my brother. But faith tests the strong. We would not be given such pain and heartache if it was not for a greater divine purpose. I believe that we are all tested for a reason. Whatever version of God you believe in, God tests our strength and our resolve. Sometimes the tests in life come before the rewards. Actually, I think that is true of most situations. That's why there is a finish line at the end. The finish line is the reward for running the race. Maybe heaven is the last finish line, and life is the test. I don't know.

Since Colin passed away, the shift I felt in my life is a result of it taking on a new inspired purpose. Now I am determined to share my story in the hopes of inspiring others to do the same. I am not ashamed of all that I have been through, the wins and the losses. I may not be able to avoid the valuables slipping out of my bag altogether, but I hope to turn the loss and pain toward the greater good. For those of us who are survivors of whatever battle we have been given, now is the time to speak up. Silence and shame only perpetuate a situation. We overcome our obstacles only by shedding light on them; we shed light by speaking out. Pain keeps us in silence, but it doesn't have to forever. We all have stories to tell that may affect others' lives in positive ways. Colin's death forever changed my life.

It has made me more resilient. It has motivated and inspired me to tell my story to help change the lives of others.

I used to think that my story didn't matter. Who am I to tell my story? I'm not rich or famous. The fact is that we all matter, no matter what we have or don't have. We all have important stories to tell. My story is just one in the many pieces of life's puzzle. I am on a mission to give a voice to the voiceless and a face to the shame of domestic abuse. I want to build a legacy to honor my grandmother and Colin for my daughters and for future generations.

Do you have a story to tell? Is your fear or shame holding you back from telling it? I am here to encourage and inspire you to share your triumphs and tragedies. There may be someone who can benefit from what you have to say. You never know whose life you can change as a result of being courageous and sharing what is inside of you.

AFFIRMATION: I am living every day to its fullest and cherishing those around me. I do not take a single minute for granted.

Exercise

* Go outside and blow some bubbles. Think about what you are grateful for and about Colin. Tell someone that you care about him or her. Don't take a single minute for granted.
* Think about how a loss has changed you and your life. Try to think about what it has taught you and what you can be grateful for out of the situation.
* Share your story. If you are scared, share it with a close friend at first. You may find that you feel free once you do.

Afterword
The Silver Lining

THE THIRTEEN YEARS THAT FOLLOWED the break from Will, my former husband and the father of my children, were spent focused and devoted to one thing: teaching my daughters what healthy relationships look like. I thought that this would be the best way to break a cycle and pattern of abusive relationships. I spent years taking my daughters to counseling and many more hours talking with them and shedding tears, showing them my mistakes and vulnerability. I took on this task of prevention wholeheartedly. The last thing I wanted as a mother was for one of my daughters to go through the same form of hell I went through.

Our discussions were at first very lighthearted and superficial while the girls were small. Then, as time went by, discussions went deeper. The three of us spent time in the counselor's office poring over issues surrounding their lives and histories while creating strategies for them to create dialogue with their father about his choices. I was feeling good. I felt like I was being proactive about their mental health and awareness around dysfunctional relationships.

During this thirteen-year time period, Will remarried and had another roller-coaster relationship of explosive fights and periods of making up. Will and his new wife would fight, she would move out, and then two days later she would be back in the house. One day my daughters left for school, and by the time they came home, the house was completely void of furniture, which left them shocked and confused. During the making-up periods, he would feel so bad that he would take them on lavish vacations. As the girls got older, they began to see this for what it was: overcompensation and guilt for the explosive marital relationship with his new wife.

I tried my hardest as a mother to combat the dark forces that surrounded my daughters' lives outside my four walls. Keeping a close relationship with both of them and fostering mutual love and respect was my approach to parenting. I was strict when it came to the what's, who's, and where's when the girls went somewhere with friends, but we would laugh and joke about me "just doing my job."

About six months before I finished writing this book, I got a call from Will early one morning. He was awakened at 2:00 a.m. by a knock on his door from two police officers. My oldest daughter's ex-boyfriend was outside soaking wet, along with the officers. The boy had been stalking my daughter and was attempting to coerce her to go outside and talk. That early morning, the boy was ticketed for criminal trespass and issued a warning for stalking. My worst nightmare had been realized. My precious daughter was involved in a relationship just like mine.

Based upon my past, I went into instant protective-mother mode with zero tolerance. I went to my daughter's high school and got the administration and the school safety officer involved. I felt fierce for my daughter's sake. I had no idea what this young man was intending or was capable of. The young man was spoken to and warned about his behavior at school. After that, my daughter had to be escorted to class by a police officer, which embarrassed her. She was humiliated by the way I handled the situation. From her perspective, her life was ruined. She and this young man were involved in groups and had a few classes together so school got a bit awkward for a while and she withdrew from her activities. She thought I overreacted, and maybe I did. But the truth is, given the level of violence that we hear about in schools today, I don't think that you can ever be too careful. After a few months of my daughter's self-inflicted isolation, she returned to her activities at school and was no longer troubled by the young man.

Out of this incident and the days that followed, Will and I talked more than we had in years. One morning I got up the courage to call him and bring up our own dark past and that day on May 21, 2002. "I really need to talk to you about our past and all of the incidents that happened. I am not angry with you nor am I judging you, but in order for me to fully heal, I need to talk about what happened thirteen years ago."

"I'm not ready to talk to you about that." He replied.

Picking up the phone that morning after all of those years to finally face talk directly to him about that day was a big courageous step for me. I could have just thrown up at that moment. Never did I think I would be having this conversation with him. I felt like I had gone back in time and faced my attacker—without anger or resentment, in a soft, peaceful way. I was ready to talk to him on my own terms and in my own time. I felt empowered.

If you had told me thirteen years ago that I would ever be able to have a peaceful al beit short conversation with my ex about what had happened, I would have told you that such a conversation would never be possible. Never did I think I could forgive him and speak about him without loathing in my heart; because of the pain he caused the girls and me. The word "forgiveness" is a big deal that I don't take lightly unless I truly feel ready to forgive.

During those twelve years, my self-inflicted isolation from my family was out of embarrassment and fear. Somehow I had it in my mind that because of what I had put them through, especially my father, they would judge me. It was easier to keep my distance. I thought it was to protect them from harm but really it was to protect my feelings out of fear of being judged and ridiculed for my choices. I learned in all of this that I had to forgive myself first in order to be able to forgive others. True forgiveness takes time and so does emotional healing.

What part of you do you need to forgive so that you can be healed of emotional scars? The truth is that healing can happen if you let it. The part of me that was ashamed is finally a closed wound. My shame has turned to power and my silence has turned into a megaphone. Some scars remain, but my heart and my soul finally feel free. My voice is ready to be heard.

Resources

1-800-799-7233 (National Domestic Violence Hotline)

Nomore.org. NO MORE is a unifying symbol and movement to raise public awareness and engage bystanders around ending domestic violence and sexual assault. Launched in March 2013 by a coalition of leading advocacy groups, service providers, the US Department of Justice, and major corporations, NO MORE is supported by hundreds of national and local groups and by thousands of individuals, organizations, universities, and communities who are using its signature blue symbol to increase visibility for domestic violence and sexual assault.

NO MORE was conceived to amplify the power of the domestic-violence and sexual-assault movement using a unifying symbol to drive awareness and break down the barriers of stigma, silence, and shame that keep people from talking about these issues and taking action to prevent them. Cofounded as a public-private partnership, NO MORE was created as a platform for those working to end domestic violence and sexual assault, in the belief that greater dialogue will fuel enhanced funding for direct service, advocacy, and prevention.

Ncadv.org. The National Coalition Against Domestic Violence (NCADV), has worked to educate and create programming and technical assistance, to assist the public in addressing the issue, and to support those impacted by domestic violence.

They provide programming and assistance through legislature and cosmetic surgery, and they honor those who have lost their lives to domestic violence.

Nrcdv.org. The NRCDV strives to be a trusted national leader and sustainable organization, renowned for innovation, multidisciplinary approaches, and a commitment to ensuring that policy, practice, and research are grounded in and guided by the voices and experiences of domestic-violence survivors and advocates.

Breakthecycle.org. Break the Cycle is the leading national nonprofit organization working to provide comprehensive dating-abuse programs exclusively to young people. Whether through designing innovative violence-prevention programs, hosting public campaigns, or championing effective laws and policies, they inspire and support young people to build healthy relationships and create a culture without abuse.

Break the Cycle was founded in Los Angeles, California, in 1996. While there were a lot of services for children experiencing abuse by adults and for adults in peer-to-peer abusive relationships, there was a gap in services for young people experiencing abuse in dating relationships. We began to fill that gap by creating teen-specific violence-prevention education and providing legal services for youth. In 2004, Break the Cycle expanded nationally in response to the need for dating-abuse services and programs. Break the Cycle now has staff in Los Angeles, California, and in the District of Columbia, along with partners, volunteers, and supporters across the nation.

About the Author

DR. AMY CANNATTA HAS TAKEN her success strategies in this book and turned them into an inspirational keynote presentation and practical coaching and mentoring program for female entrepreneurs who are ready to bring their big dreams to life and build financial freedom. Her coaching clients have experienced dramatic personal transformation, substantial increases in their income, healthier and more vibrant living, while mastering their confidence. Dr. Cannatta has also worked with women for tv and media appearances. She is a Cum Laude graduate from the University of Bridgeport, College of Chiropractic. She is a collaborative author of the #1 International Amazon Best Seller, *Chocolate and Diamonds for the Woman's Soul* and nationally published in the April 2015 edition of My Menopause magazine. To learn more, visit her website at www.amycannatta.com or by email at admin@amycannatta.com

39179225R00097

Made in the USA
Middletown, DE
14 March 2019